Secrets of

COLOR HEALING

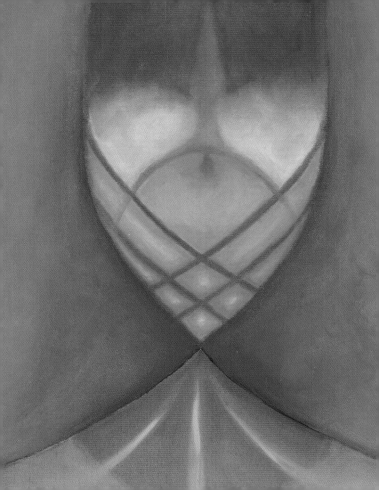

Secrets of
COLOR
HEALING

STEPHANIE NORRIS

DK Publishing, Inc.

DK

LONDON, NEW YORK, SYDNEY, DELHI, PARIS,
MUNICH, and JOHANNESBURG

This book was conceived, designed, and produced by
THE IVY PRESS LIMITED,
The Old Candlemakers,
Lewes, East Sussex BN7 2NZ

Art director Peter Bridgewater
Publisher Sophie Collins
Editorial director Steve Luck
Designers Kevin Knight, Jane Lanaway
Project editor Caroline Earle
Picture researcher Vanessa Fletcher, Trudi Valter
Photography Guy Ryecart
Illustrators Kim Glass, Sarah Young, Andrew Kulman, Ivan Hissey,
Michael Courteney, Catherine McIntyre
Three-dimensional models Mark Jamieson

First published in The United States of America in 2001 by
DK PUBLISHING, INC.
95 Madison Avenue, New York, New York 10016

Copyright © 2001 The Ivy Press Limited

A Cataloging-in-Publication record is available
from the Library of Congress
ISBN 0-7894-7785-8

Note from the publisher
Although every effort has been made to ensure that the information
presented in this book is correct, the author and publisher cannot be
held responsible for any injuries which may arise.

Originated and printed by
Hong Kong Graphics and Printing Limited, China

see our complete
catalog at
www.dk.com

CONTENTS

Color psychology
*Discover how each color
of the spectrum can have
an effect on your moods,
emotions, and behavior.*

HOW TO USE THIS BOOK

To make *Secrets of Color Healing* easy to use it has been split into four distinct sections. The first of these describes how color was used for healing in ancient times and explains the scientific principles behind color healing. The second part focuses on the seven colors of the spectrum and their properties. The third part details the methods of color healing, giving advice on practicing color healing at home, including color visualization and color meditation. The final part looks at how color in the environment is important and how to feel in harmony with the colors we absorb in our daily lives.

Practical information
*The properties of each color are
described on colorful practical pages.*

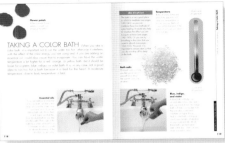

Home treatment
Practical spreads show how you can use various color treatments at home.

TAKING A COLOR BATH

Detail
Black-and-white spreads provide further information and detail.

Different Kinds of Color Baths

COLOR THAT YOU LIVE WITH

Environment
Learn how the colors in your environment, including clothes and interiors, can help enhance your mental well-being.

Introduction

Survival
Color has played a vital part in human health, survival, and culture since ancient times.

Color is, quite simply, light, and none of us can live without it. The cells of our bodies react to it, or the lack of it, and this affects directly our physical, emotional, mental, and spiritual well-being. We have only to think of how we intuitively respond to color—such as with awe at the splendor of a sunrise, or with hope at the magic of a rainbow—to realize its power to heal.

The first color healers

Our primitive ancestors were much more in touch with the healing properties of color than we are today. From their observation of nature and the world around them, they learned to attribute certain properties to certain colors and these properties still hold good today. For instance red was the color of the precious fire that warmed their bodies and over which they cooked their food; it was also the color of the blood that ran through their veins. Red was therefore the color of life and so figured prominently in their art and rituals.

Dyes and pigments

Dark blue, or indigo, was the color of the sky under which they slept and dreamed at night to awake refreshed to another day. And green was the color of the wild plants that they sought out for food or as medicine when they were sick or wounded.

Our ancestors also used color in the form of natural dyes extracted from plants. This was employed to decorate their bodies. Pigments were also made from ground minerals or crushed berries and used to paint the walls of the caves in which they lived.

The color of the environment

We too express ourselves through the color we wear and the colors with which we decorate our home environment. We are also instinctively drawn to the particular colors that we require in order to correct an imbalance of energy in ourselves, which may be resulting in physical, mental, or emotional problems. By eating, wearing, or surrounding ourselves with the color—exposing ourselves to it in some way—we heal ourselves. This is the very essence of color healing and is part of the ancient wisdom that we have begun to return to in the New Age.

Electromagnetic Spectrum

White light is made up of many different colors, of which the human eye can only see about 40 percent. Each color has a different wavelength and vibrational frequency. The electromagnetic waves we cannot see are radio waves, infrared, ultraviolet, X rays, and gamma waves. Some people believe we are capable of seeing colors outside our normal range by using our "third eye" (see page 37).

HISTORY OF
COLOR HEALING

Color healing has its roots in the ancient civilizations of Egypt, India, and China, and even lost Atlantis. In the circular temples of Atlantis there are reputed to have been special chambers where people went to be healed by a combination of natural light and crystals. ∼ The temples of the ancient Egyptians were likewise constructed to channel the rays of the sun for healing purposes. The great cathedrals of the Middle Ages were similarly fitted with stained-glass windows, through which the sun cast pools of colored light in which the weak and sick could bathe and have their health restored. ∼ Humanity has always worshiped the sun—its light contains all the colors of the spectrum and has been known for its healing properties since ancient times.

The Doctrine of Humors

Color treatment
The great physicians of ancient times, including Avicenna, used color to treat the various ills of their patients.

Throughout the Middle Ages the treatment of disease, or imbalance in the body, was led by the *Doctrine of Humors*. According to this doctrine there were four main bodily fluids or humors—blood, phlegm, choler (bile), and black choler. These corresponded to the four astrological elements—Fire, Earth, Air, and Water (see pages 30–33)—and were associated with the qualities of heat, dryness, coldness, and moisture.

Each humor also related to a particular color and constitution or temperament. Therefore, an excess of red blood meant that the person was considered to be of a sanguine or cheerful and optimistic disposition; if white phlegm was dominant, then the person was stolid in nature; yellow bile meant that the person was quick to anger or irascible; black bile denoted a person of melancholy disposition.

Avicenna

It was believed that if the humors were out of proportion to one another in the body, treatment using the relevant color (see below) could bring them back into balance.

This type of color therapy was known to physicians of ancient times too; the Persian physician, Avicenna (980–1037), wrote in his influential *Canon of Medicine* that red stimulated the circulation of the blood. So, someone who was bleeding should not look at anything red; rather he or she should look upon blue because it had a calming effect, reducing the flow of blood. Accordingly, he prescribed (inspired by the work of great philosophers and physicians such as

Aristotle, Pythagoras, and Hippocrates) colored ointments, bandages, and flowers in his treatment of disease.

Paracelsus

One of the best-known physicians of the Renaissance period was a Swiss who called himself Paracelsus (1493–1541). He was a man possessed of remarkable healing talents and used color in his treatment of patients. He also used herbs, music, and many of the other alternative or complementary medicines that are gaining in popularity today. However, his name meant "greater than Celsus," the famous physician of ancient Rome, and his outspoken attitude to the authorities of the day made him many enemies. During his lifetime his work was not given the recognition it deserved.

Hippocrates

Hippocrates (c. 460–c. 377 BC) defined man according to the four elements, relating male to Fire (red) and Air (yellow), female to Earth (green) and Water (blue).

Crystal light
A crystal refracts light into the colors of the spectrum in much the same way as a prism.

DISCOVERING COLOR

The great English mathematician and physicist, Sir Isaac Newton (1642–1727) is best known for his formulation of the laws of gravity, but he also discovered how the color spectrum is produced. This discovery came about quite accidentally when Cambridge University was closed down during the Great Plague and he was forced to continue his studies at home. Newton's work forms the basis of today's understanding of color.

Newton
Newton's scientific theory of refraction is spectacularly demonstrated in nature by the phenomenon of the rainbow.

Blue

Indigo

Violet

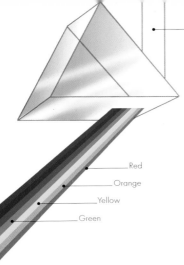

White light is refracted, forming the spectrum of seven colors, when it passes through a prism

Red

Orange

Yellow

Green

Newton's prism

While working at home on understanding the nature of light, Newton experimented with passing the sunlight that entered his room through a prism. It was then that he discovered that the light was refracted or deflected into the colors of the spectrum.

When he experimented further, he found that each color had a different angle of refraction and this is what made it visible to the human eye as red, orange, yellow, and so on. He also found that if he turned the prism upside down, the colors combined to form white light again.

Newton concluded that light, or color, consists of waves, and each color has a different wavelength and vibrates at a different frequency. This is how he arrived at what we now know is the scientific explanation of color.

D.P. Ghadiali

It was a Hindu scientist, D.P. Ghadiali (1873–1966), working in the United States in the early part of the twentieth century, who formulated the scientific principles behind the effects the different colors have on the human body. He found that for each organism or system there was a particular color that stimulated, and another that inhibited, its functioning. It therefore followed that if a part of the body was not functioning normally, balance could be restored by treatment with the appropriate color.

Edwin Babbitt and Rudolf Steiner

Steiner
*Rudolf Steiner's ideas on color
are still used in schools today
to encourage children to learn.*

One of the most important pioneers of color healing was the American Edwin D. Babbitt (1828–1905). His magnum opus, *The Principles of Light and Color*, caused quite a stir when published in 1878. In his book Babbitt described the different healing effects of the colors of the spectrum and identified red as stimulating the blood, blue as calming it, and orange and yellow as useful for stimulating the nerves. Accordingly, Babbitt prescribed treatment with red

for paralysis; blue for inflammatory and nervous conditions; and yellow to act as a laxative.

Babbitt invented various devices for treatment with color including the Chromalume, a kind of cabinet in which the patient sat, exposed to the light of the sun, in order to be bathed in color from a window made of colored glass. Many of Babbitt's devices were originally banned, but still served as prototypes for aids to color treatment that are used today.

Rudolf Steiner

The Austrian philosopher, mystic, and educationist, Rudolf Steiner (1861–1925), used color in his spiritual teachings. Although educated as a scientist, from an early age Steiner experienced a spiritual reality that could not be explained in terms of the material world. Later he founded Anthroposophy, a movement that seeks to develop people's spiritual perception and understanding of themselves in relation to the universe. This led to the founding of Steiner schools.

Steiner's first center for spiritual learning, the *Goetheanum* in Dornach, in Switzerland, had colored glass windows to help people become aware of the different effects of color. Blue brought a sense of peace, green a feeling of harmony, violet enhanced self-respect, and rose gave rise to feelings of unconditional love. In Steiner schools today this use of color is reflected at every stage of a child's development, with bright, warm colors for the young, and cooler colors for older children.

Steiner and Goethe

Steiner was influenced by J.W. von Goethe (1749–1832), the great German writer. Goethe mounted a crusade against Newton and his scientific theory of color (see pages 14–15), arguing that colors were seen by the eye according to prevailing conditions and were a combination of light and darkness. Goethe's theory did not convince scientists.

Healing gods
Ancient gods and goddesses of healing have inspired the color therapists of today.

THEO GIMBEL can be described as the elder statesman of modern color therapy, particularly in Britain. A Bavarian who has made his home in Britain, Gimbel has been much influenced by the work of Goethe and Steiner. However, he has formulated his own unique approach to color therapy, following on from ancient esoteric teachings.

Color pioneer
It was Gimbel's experiences as a prisoner of war in Russia, and later as a teacher of mentally handicapped children, that led him to develop a lifelong interest in the effects of color. After many years of research, he founded the Hygeia College of Color Therapy, which was named, appropriately, after the Greek goddess of health. At this college Gimbel has trained many of the color therapists practicing today. Gimbel was influenced by Goethe and this picture shows a table of color refraction from one of Goethe's works on color: *Zur Farbenlehre.*

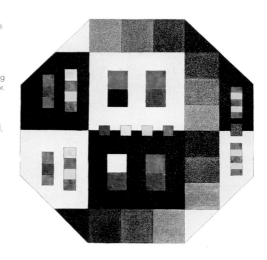

Gimbel sees color as part of a continuum beginning with darkness and light and progressing to sound and form. He is particularly well known for his method of spinal diagnosis. When he was young he broke his spine and might well have suffered permanent immobility if it had not been for the wisdom of a family doctor, who decided not to put him in a cast but to let him lie in bed and then to encourage him in gentle exercise. In Gimbel's method, patients have a chart of the spine drawn, which they then sign. The signature contains the patient's energy, which a healer is able to pick up. Then each vertebra is dowsed (see pages 106–107), the chart interpreted, and a color selected for treatment. Gimbel has developed his own color therapy instrument that exposes the patient at precisely timed intervals to a color and its complementary color (see pages 92–93).

Spinal diagnosis
Using Gimbel's method the patient signs a drawing of his or her spine. Then each vertebra is dowsed to find the appropriate color for treatment.

History of Color Healing **Theo Gimbel**

SECRETS OF COLOR HEALING

Modern Applications of Color

Environment

Color is used in different environments, including schools, to influence people to behave in certain ways.

The work of the pioneers in color healing was overshadowed by scientific and technological advances in modern medicine. But while modern medicine has long used the colors at the invisible end of the color spectrum, infrared and ultraviolet, it is only relatively recently that medical practitioners have begun to use the visible colors. Blue light, in particular, has been shown to be effective in the treatment of various diseases, both physical and psychological, including cancer, eating disorders, and various addictions.

Generally speaking, the medical profession has become much more aware of the physical and psychological effects of color. This can be seen, for example, in the choice of color for gowns worn in hospital operating theaters: green for harmony, or light blue for calmness and coolness.

Mood shifters

Other professions and institutions, such as prisons and schools, also consciously use certain colors. In prisons, the use of soft pink to paint walls has been shown to reduce the incidence of aggressive and violent behavior in inmates; while in schools yellow has been shown to stimulate learning. However, yellow is a color to be avoided in the environment of the mentally ill or highly stressed because it is possible that it will overexcite sufferers.

Artificial light

Natural light is beneficial to us, but some artificial light has been shown to have a detrimental effect on people exposed to it, whether in the office or in public places. For example, some people react adversely to fluorescent light because it is lacking in the colors at the blue end of the spectrum and has a fast flicker. It has been shown to cause headaches and stress.

Photobiologist Dr. John Ott developed the full-spectrum tube that is in use in many offices today. This provides a close equivalent of daylight, and is therefore much healthier.

Theo Gimbel (see pages 18–19) has done extensive research into sodium street lighting, showing that it creates a negative environment that can lead to depression and crime. He advocates the installation of street lighting that is made up of light toward the blue end of the spectrum, in order to reduce stress and violent behavior.

COLORS OF
THE SPECTRUM

Light, more specifically the colors that are visible to the human eye, actually occupies only a small part of the electromagnetic spectrum. This spectrum includes infrared light at one end and ultraviolet light at the other, which we cannot see. It also includes X rays, gamma rays, radio waves, and microwaves; the latter two are so-called because, like the rest of the spectrum, this kind of energy radiates out in waves. ➤ The distance from one crest of a wave to another—known as the wavelength—determines what kind of wave it is. The wavelength varies depending on the color, the longest being at the red end and the shortest at the violet end. These seven colors—red, orange, yellow, green, blue, indigo, and violet—are also known as the seven rays.

How We React to Color

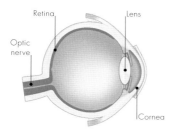

The eye

Light enters our bodies through the eye, where the light-sensitive retina breaks it down into color.

Just as the colors of the spectrum can be produced by directing sunlight through a prism (see pages 14–15), so a rainbow is created when the rays of the sun are refracted through drops of rain. The larger the drops, the brighter the colors.

The lens of the eye similarly acts to refract or change the direction of light, focusing it on the retina, which is the light-sensitive membrane found at the back of the eye. There the light then stimulates two kinds of cells, known as rod cells and cone cells. Rod cells are sensitive to dim light, enabling us to distinguish between light and shade, and day and night, while cone cells are sensitive to the wavelengths of the three primary colors, red, green, and blue. When light hits these cells it triggers nerve impulses that are transmitted via the optic nerve to the brain, where the image is then formed. And that is how we see color.

Color, hormones, and behavior

Color produces a biochemical reaction within our bodies, directly stimulating important glands, like the pituitary gland for instance, which is the master gland of the endocrine system. This gland produces the hormones that regulate our bodily functions—our sleep patterns, sex drive, metabolic rate, appetite, and so on—as well as our moods, emotions, and behavior. Two of the most important hormones are melatonin and serotonin, and these are both secreted by the pineal gland, which is located in the brain. The production of serotonin is stimulated by day and the production of melatonin by night. Serotonin has an uplifting effect, helping us to stay awake and be alert, while melatonin has a sedative effect, aiding sleep.

SAD

High levels of melatonin have been found in people suffering from SAD, or Seasonal Affective Disorder. This is a specific type of depression that many people suffer from in the winter months due to lack of sunlight. Some of the symptoms include the desire to sleep, general fatigue, and a lack of interest in sex. However, such people have been found to respond dramatically to treatment with full-spectrum white light.

Genetic Programming

This direct response to the lack of color in winter is thought to be held deep in our genetic memory. This goes back to the time when, like animals, we hibernated in winter due to the necessity to survive when the weather was extreme and food was scarce.

Purple prose
"Purple prose" describes flowery language, in which the writer gets carried away.

THE PSYCHOLOGY OF COLOR

The profound effect color has on our moods, emotions, and behavior is reflected in the sayings that pepper our everyday language. We unconsciously resort to these to describe how we are feeling or to explain our reaction to something. Their use of colors that everyone can relate to easily makes them an extremely effective form of communication.

Green with envy
To be "green with jealousy or envy" is to be emotionally out of balance—green is the color that holds the balance between the warm or red end of the color spectrum and the cool or blue end.

The blues
When we say we have "the blues," we are communicating that we are in solitary, introverted mode.

Seeing red

When we say we "see red" or "it was like a red rag to a bull," we are describing a response that is invariably immediate and involves anger or aggression. This is something that is very deeply ingrained in us. If our ancestors had not met the threat of danger with the will to fight or the strength and speed to run away—the so-called "fight-or-flight" response—we would not have evolved to the present day.

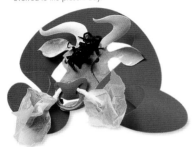

Yellow-bellied

"Yellow" or "yellow-bellied" is often used to describe a coward, someone who will not move to defend himself or someone else.

Black dog

A "colorful character" is someone who has lived a full and interesting life; "colorful language" often includes words of the four-letter variety into which a lot of physical energy is usually put. By contrast, we talk about the "black dog of depression," using black to describe a world from which all color, or life, seems to have disappeared.

Color and Personality

Color you like
*The colors that you choose
say a lot about the kind of person
you are and what you like.*

We all have preferences for one color or another and these colors say a lot about us, psychologically as well as physically. A Swiss professor of psychology, Max Lüscher, is famous for developing a test for analyzing people's color preferences according to their personality type.

In the Lüscher Color Test people were asked to select a range of colors in order of preference. Someone who chose red was likely to be assertive or aggressive, strong-willed, and confident, of the "red" personality type; on the other hand, someone who chose blue was likely to be shy or usually held themselves aloof, of the "blue" personality type.

There is now some controversy over the colors Lüscher chose for his test—he included brown, gray, and black, which are not colors of the spectrum—and other, more modern tests have since been devised. It is also true to say that a red personality type, someone with high blood pressure, say, or a quick temper, is just as likely to avoid the color and opt for its cooling opposite, blue, instead. The colors we like are often the colors we instinctively know we need.

Color is personal

Our choice of color is intensely personal; the clothes we wear, the decor of our homes, even the car we drive, are all making personal statements about ourselves. When we decide to change our color scheme—paint a room a different color, or wear a different color—we are saying something different about ourselves, whether we know it or not.

It is important to wear, or have around you, the colors you like—they will have a positive effect on you. A color may have a special meaning for you because it is associated with a happy memory, perhaps from childhood. If you now live in the city, for example, but were brought up in the country, you may long for the sight of green fields. A walk in the countryside may be just what you need to refresh yourself after the stress of city life. Or, failing that, try hanging pictures of landscapes on the walls in which the color green predominates.

Dowsing for Color

If you are not sure what color you need in your life right now, try dowsing to find out (see pages 106–107). Once you know, you will discover that you start attracting it to yourself— it will suddenly leap out at you, in the dress or shirt that someone is wearing, in an advertisement on a billboard, or even in a certain fruit on a market stall.

ASTROLOGY AND COLOR

There are 12 signs of the zodiac, 10 planets, and 4 elements (Fire, Earth, Air, and Water). Fire is associated with the color red, Earth with green, Water with blue, and Air with yellow or light blue. The signs of the zodiac are divided into Fire, Earth, Air, or Water signs (see pages 32–33). The planets are positioned in the signs. An astrologer can calculate your birthchart and discover what planets you have in the signs or elements, in order to determine which colors dominate and which are lacking.

MOON

The Sun
 The masculine or active energy, the Sun is a bright golden yellow, a hot and fierce energy that it is dangerous to expose yourself to for too long.

Mercury
The planet of the mind and communication, is usually depicted as light blue or yellow, the color of the intellect.

Mars
The planet of action, aggression, and war, is an unequivocal red.

MARS

The Moon
On the other hand, the Moon is the feminine or receptive energy. It is a silvery white, and in its radiance we can seek to escape the everyday world and aspire to a different kind of reality.

Ancient and Modern

The most important of the ten planets are the Sun and the Moon, also known as the Lights or Luminaries.

In addition to the planets Mercury, Venus, and Mars, in ancient or traditional astrology there were two more planets: Jupiter and Saturn.

Modern astrology has added three more planets, discovered in more recent times: Uranus, Neptune, and Pluto.

Venus
The planet of love, beauty, and the arts, Venus is green, which is the color of growth, fecundity, and balance.

Uranus
This planet rules new ideas, especially those that challenge the status quo, and is sky blue.

Neptune
This planet rules all things watery, emotional, and spiritual, and is, as you would expect, a deep blue.

Jupiter
The planet of expansion and good fortune, is purple.

Pluto
This planet controls all the things we do not want to know about—repressed emotions, dark secrets, and compulsions—and is, of course, black.

SATURN

NEPTUNE

Saturn
The planet of work, responsibility, and duty, which, appropriately, is brown or black.

The Elements

Planets
The number of planets you have in the elements tells you what color you lack.

The 12 signs of the zodiac fall into four groups of three, which are divided by element:
• **The Fire signs** Aries, Leo, and Sagittarius.
• **The Earth signs** Taurus, Virgo, and Capricorn.
• **The Air signs** Gemini, Libra, and Aquarius.
• **The Water signs** Cancer, Pisces, and Scorpio.
Each of these groups has its own distinguishing characteristics, both negative and positive. The Fire signs are noted for their energy, spontaneity, intuition, and belief in themselves, but they can also be egotistical and overbearing. If your birthchart shows that you have a lot of planets in Fire, you have a lot of red energy.

The Earth signs tend to be sensual, productive, conservative, and grounded in the material world. However, they can also be unimaginative and narrow-minded. If you have a lot of planets in the Earth element, you have a lot of green energy.

The Air signs are intelligent, communicative, sociable, and at home in the world of ideas; they can also be malicious and unfeeling. If you have a lot of planets in Air, then you have a lot of (light) blue or yellow energy.

The Water signs are sensitive, emotional, imaginative, and need to experience a soul or spiritual connection with others. However, they also tend to be melodramatic and irrational. If you have a lot of planets in Water, then you have a lot of (dark) blue energy.

The missing element

It is quite common to have very few planets, or even none at all, in one of the elements, which then becomes your missing element. For example, if you have no planets in Fire, then that means that you are lacking red energy; if you have no planets in Water, then you are lacking blue energy.

You can also have an excess of certain elements. If you have a "red" planet like Mars in one of the Fire signs, it can give you an excess of red energy, while having a lot of the planets in the Air signs can give you an excess of (light) blue/yellow energy.

Once you have all this vital information you can then choose to surround yourself with the colors you need to balance your energies.

Astrology

Astrology links the movements of the planets to events on Earth, allowing the astrologer to predict what is likely to happen in a person's life. The signs of the zodiac relate to the twelve 30° sectors in the Sun's annual path.

Balance of color

Being healthy means balancing the color energies of different parts of the body.

THE SEVEN RAYS These

are the seven visible colors of the spectrum—
red, orange, yellow, green, blue, indigo, and
violet. The seven rays correspond to the seven chakras or energy centers in the
body (see pages 100–101). On a spiritual level, they symbolize great cosmic
forces that represent different evolutionary stages in the history of humanity.

Evolution

We are currently
thought to be evolving
from the red end of
the spectrum to the
blue end, which is
associated more
with the higher
manifestation of our
being. It is interesting
to note in this respect
our growing concern
with green or
environmental issues
and the growth of the
ecological movement
and political parties
concerned with
green issues.

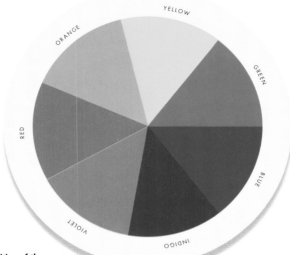

RED · ORANGE · YELLOW · GREEN · BLUE · INDIGO · VIOLET

Qualities of the rays

The seven rays are also associated with different qualities, which we all have to a greater or lesser degree. A few people are only of one ray and they are then said to be "on" the blue ray or whatever; most of us are a mixture of rays.

Ray Keywords		
Color	**Positive**	**Negative**
Red	Strength	Brutality
Orange	Acceptance	Indifference
Yellow	Intellect	Coldness
Green	Empathy	Self-absorption
Blue	Justice	Intolerance
Indigo	Devotion	Self-delusion
Violet	Mysticism	Arrogance

Properties of the Rays

Type of person
*The color of the energy you have helps
to define what type of person you are
both physically and psychologically.*

The rays have both physical and
psychological attributes. Those
at the red or warm end of the
spectrum are more physical, and reflect
the way in which we express ourselves
outwardly, while those at the blue or
cool end are more psychological, and
echo our inner selves.

The warm rays

The red ray correlates with the base
chakra at the root of the spine and this
stimulates our physical vitality, which is
particularly important for the procreative
functions of the body. It is also
associated with the qualities of strength,
will, and courage.

The orange ray helps the assimilative
and digestive processes of the body
and it relates to the second or navel
chakra. People with a lot of orange
energy are healthy in mind and body,
always think positively, and are
physically active.

Yellow is the ray of the intellect and
its chakra is situated at the solar plexus,
an important center for the nervous
system. The yellow ray is associated
with the qualities of intelligence,
rationality, and the ability to
concentrate and focus.

Green is in the middle of the
spectrum and is the color of the heart
chakra in the middle of the chest. This
is the ray of harmony and balance,
sympathy, compassion, and devotion.

The cool rays

Blue is the first of the cool colors of the
spectrum, and these rays counter or
slow down the warm colors. This end

of the spectrum takes us inward and upward, away from the physical and toward the spiritual. Blue relates to the throat chakra—the center of speech—and its qualities are truth, sincerity, and reflectiveness.

The indigo ray takes us higher still, into the realms controlled by the brow chakra, or third eye. This enables us to see in the psychic sense, discerning things not perceived by the five senses. The qualities of this ray are vision, inspiration, and service to humanity.

Violet is the last of the colors of the spectrum and people on this ray are at a high level of consciousness. It is the ray of the crown chakra, situated on top of the head, and its qualities are spirituality, mysticism, and the expression of the higher self.

Chakras and Color Healing

Chakras are energy centers in the body, and if they are not functioning properly, they can detrimentally affect well-being. Each chakra is associated with a color, so any imbalance should be treated using the relevant color.

Red rose
A red rose symbolizes passion and is habitually given to the one we love.

RED

Red is the color of life itself, of fire and of blood, of danger, and sex, and without it our lives would lack vigor, warmth, strength, and passion. We need it in the food we eat, the clothes we wear, and our physical surroundings in order to stimulate our nervous system, release epinephrine into the blood, and improve our circulation. We also need red to root ourselves in everyday reality and to give us a sense of security.

A red rag to a bull
Red is a very physical color and often provokes a physical reaction, sometimes violent. Perhaps one of the reasons English soccer fans have a reputation as troublemakers is that the English soccer team wear red shirts and the cross of St. George on the English flag is also red!

Saint George
St. George slaying the dragon illustrates the strength, courage, and aggression that are associated with red.

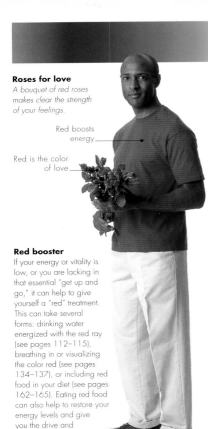

Roses for love

A bouquet of red roses makes clear the strength of your feelings.

Red boosts energy

Red is the color of love

Red booster

If your energy or vitality is low, or you are lacking in that essential "get up and go," it can help to give yourself a "red" treatment. This can take several forms: drinking water energized with the red ray (see pages 112–115), breathing in or visualizing the color red (see pages 134–137), or including red food in your diet (see pages 162–165). Eating red food can also help to restore your energy levels and give you the drive and motivation to achieve your goals.

Cautions

Red is a very powerful color and should not be used if you suffer from high blood pressure or heart problems, have a quick temper, or are feeling angry or upset because it will only overstimulate you. You should also be aware that treatment with red should always be complemented by treatment with blue or green (see pages 92–93).

Healing with Red

Treatment with red can benefit the following conditions:

PHYSICAL CONDITIONS

low energy

anemia

poor circulation

low blood pressure

colds/chills

NEGATIVE STATES OF MIND

apathy

depression

fear

lack of confidence/initiative

Using the Color Red

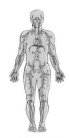

Lifeblood
Red is the color of the lifeblood that flows through our veins and circulates round our bodies.

Red is the color of the element of Fire, the element of the signs of the zodiac Aries, Leo, and Sagittarius (see pages 32–33) and is particularly associated with the planet Mars, which is known as "the red planet." Mars rules aggression and sex drive and the part of the body that the color red relates to is the genitals. It is therefore a good color to wear if your libido is low or you want to spice up your sex life!

One of the main attributes of the color red is passion, the zest for life as well as sexual passion. We give red roses to the one we love, and Valentine's Day is characterized by a flurry of red hearts on cards and giftware. In this context, too, red can also be a euphemism—an insalubrious part of a town is usually known as "the red-light district."

People on the red ray, or those with a lot of red energy, tend to be positive, confident, and optimistic about the future. They usually look forward to the day ahead and face obstacles with courage and strength. However, they can also express their "red" traits more negatively, by selfishly pursuing their own ends without regard for the feelings of others.

Affirmations

If you are feeling at a low ebb, either physically or emotionally, and want to give yourself a boost, it can help to practice one of the color healing treatments described on pages 38–39.

You can also write yourself a "red" affirmation. Affirmations are simple sentences, best written in the present

Red Affirmation

"I have the energy, the will, and the confidence to face whatever the day brings."

tense, which affirm or positively reinforce a state of being. They can be spoken while looking into a mirror, so that the words are reflected back at you, increasing their power and helping you to absorb and act on your affirmation. Alternatively, the words can be written down on a piece of paper and put under your pillow when you go to bed at night.

If you repeat your affirmation often enough, or continue to keep the piece of paper under your pillow night after night, your subconscious mind is likely to receive the message it contains and will react accordingly.

Red Keywords

Positive energetic, enthusiastic, assertive, spontaneous, strong-willed, courageous, self-motivated

Negative insensitive, aggressive, impatient, domineering, self-centered

Calendula
The orange, daisy-like flowers of calendula cannot fail to bring cheer.

ORANGE
On the color wheel orange falls between red and yellow and it therefore acts on both the physical body (red) and the intellect (yellow). Like red, it is a strong and vibrant color and needs to be used with care. We associate orange with health and vitality. Many people start the day with a glass of orange juice, which has a tonic effect and is full of the vitamin C that is needed to boost the immune system and ward off colds and illnesses.

Youth and activity
Orange is the color of youth and activity, and schoolchildren are often given oranges to eat at recess during phys. ed.

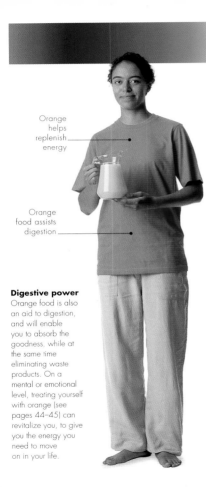

Orange
helps
replenish
energy

Orange
food assists
digestion

Digestive power
Orange food is also
an aid to digestion,
and will enable
you to absorb the
goodness, while at
the same time
eliminating waste
products. On a
mental or emotional
level, treating yourself
with orange (see
pages 44–45) can
revitalize you, to give
you the energy you
need to move
on in your life.

Cautions

You have no need of extra
orange if you are fit and well
and enjoying life. Too much
orange and you may become
complacent or self-indulgent.
Like red, orange is a strong
color and needs to be
used with care.

Healing with Orange

Treatment with orange can
benefit the following conditions:

PHYSICAL CONDITIONS

low vitality/appetite

indigestion

asthma

cramps

gallstones

NEGATIVE STATES OF MIND

Listlessness

bereavement

inhibition

sadness

boredom

Using the Color Orange

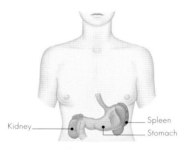

Digestive organs
The color orange is associated with the digestive and eliminative organs of the body.

Orange relates to the spleen, an organ situated behind the stomach, on the left side of the abdomen. The spleen is connected both to the stomach and the kidneys and its function is to maintain the blood, keeping it clean and healthy. The spleen breaks up worn-out red and white blood cells and also stores red blood cells for use in emergencies.

The archaic meaning of "spleen" is "the seat of the emotions." To "vent one's spleen" is to be spiteful or disagreeable in some way. And just as the organ filters out impurities from the blood, so treatment with the color orange can help you to assimilate negative feelings or come to terms with traumatic events in your life, such as the loss of someone close or the break-up of a relationship.

Orange can also be of benefit when you feel that you are in a rut, stuck in your life, and fearful of making the changes that will enable you to leave the past behind and go forward into the future. The action associated with this color is expansion, the opening up of yourself to life, so that you can engage with it once more.

Positive thinking

Orange is also associated with positive thinking and motivation, which is why it is often used in corporate colors by businesses who want to encourage us to buy certain products.

Writing an "orange" affirmation can help you to regain a sense of *joie de vivre*. It will act as a kind of mental

Orange Affirmation

"I have a healthy mind and body and enjoy life to the full."

"pick-me-up" in much the same way as drinking a glass of orange juice or water charged with orange energy (see pages 112–115) revitalizes the physical body.

It can also help to wear something orange. It doesn't have to be a complete outfit; orange is a very bright color and is therefore not suitable for everyone's skin tone, but a scarf or tie, or even a piece of amber or coral jewelry is enough to make a difference. Even a simple gesture like placing a vase of sunny calendula or striking tiger lilies in your surroundings can help to lift your mood. Try it and see how well it works.

Orange Keywords

Positive exuberant, sensual, gregarious, good-humored, playful, athletic

Negative overindulgent, lazy, dependent, unkind, superficial

Yellow flowers
*It's good to have
yellow flowers in your
environment if you are
feeling depressed.*

YELLOW
Perhaps more than any other flower, it is the daffodil that cheers us up after the long dark days of winter, its bright yellow trumpeting the arrival of spring. The poet William Wordsworth was so inspired by the sight of a bank of daffodils when he was out walking one day, that he wrote a poem about them. It begins with one of the most famous lines in the English language, "I wandered lonely as a cloud." In the poem Wordsworth speaks of how his spirits were lifted by the sight of the massed blooms, and continued to be, long after the moment had passed.

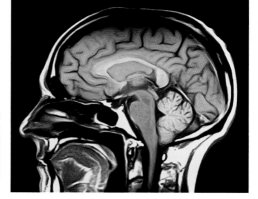

Left brain
The color yellow relates
to the rational mind and
clear thinking, associated
with the left brain, as
opposed to intuition and
clairvoyance, associated
with the right brain.

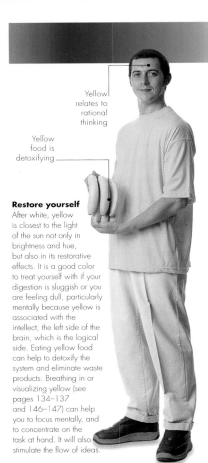

Yellow relates to rational thinking

Yellow food is detoxifying

You should avoid the color yellow if you have stomach problems, are feeling excitable or restless, are stressed or unable to "wind down," or if you have trouble sleeping.

Restore yourself

After white, yellow is closest to the light of the sun not only in brightness and hue, but also in its restorative effects. It is a good color to treat yourself with if your digestion is sluggish or you are feeling dull, particularly mentally because yellow is associated with the intellect, the left side of the brain, which is the logical side. Eating yellow food can help to detoxify the system and eliminate waste products. Breathing in or visualizing yellow (see pages 134–137 and 146–147) can help you to focus mentally, and to concentrate on the task at hand. It will also stimulate the flow of ideas.

Healing with Yellow

Treatment with yellow can benefit the following conditions:

PHYSICAL CONDITIONS

constipation

gas

diabetes

skin problems

nervous exhaustion

NEGATIVE STATES OF MIND

depression

low self-esteem

short attention span

examination nerves

writer's block

Using the Color Yellow

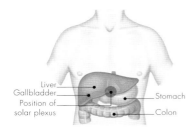

Liver
Gallbladder
Position of
solar plexus
Stomach
Colon

Solar plexus
*Linked to the liver, intestines, and
gallbladder, the network of nerves
that radiate out from the solar plexus
resembles the rays of the sun.*

Yellow relates to the solar plexus, the network of sympathetic nerves situated behind the stomach. It is linked to key abdominal organs, the liver, intestines, and gallbladder.

The solar plexus is an important center in the body for all the digestive processes and the word "solar" comes from the Latin *sol*, which means "sun," the center of the solar system.

Yellow stimulates the action of the abdominal organs, in particular the flow of bile, which plays an essential part in the digestion and absorption of fats. Bile is secreted by the liver, the chief function of which is to process what we eat into substances that the body needs.

In ancient times, the liver was considered to be the seat of love or passion, hence the expression "lily-livered," to describe a coward.

Eliminating negativity

On a psychological, as well as physical, level yellow helps get things moving, eliminating negative thoughts and feelings that can undermine our sense of self-worth.

It can also do a similar thing in social circumstances; if you want your parties to be lively affairs, try introducing some yellow into the decor of the parts of your home where people gather. Too much, though, and people are likely to become overstimulated and start arguing with each other.

Yellow is also a good color for children, since it helps to develop their cognitive abilities. If they have a playroom or study, it is beneficial to include some yellow in the room's color scheme. It is wise to avoid painting children's bedrooms in this color, however, because its stimulating qualities may cause restlessness and difficulty in sleeping.

The golden touch

Gold, or golden yellow, represents knowledge at its highest level; the wisdom gained through the assimilation of experience. In the spiritual sense this is ultimately more precious than the gold jewelry that is so often a symbol of wealth, status, and privilege.

Yellow Keywords

Positive rational, clear-thinking, broad-minded, detached, sociable

Negative critical, argumentative, opinionated, evasive, restless

Green food

Green food is essential for good health, helping to keep our bodies in balance. Avocados are a good source of vitamins A and E.

GREEN

Green is the color of nature—of the fields, hills, and woods where we often go in order to refresh ourselves and recharge our batteries after a sojourn among the buildings of town or city. In nature everything is in harmony and surrounded by it we can find our center again after a busy, stressful time at work or with family.

Green Man

The Green Man is a pagan symbol representing the growth and fecundity of nature.

The soothing power of nature

If you are feeling out of sorts, it can often help to take a walk in the countryside; if that is not possible because you live in a town or city, you can always go to a park or public gardens. Do not be afraid to hug a tree, however ridiculous you think it may look; trees are great reservoirs of energy and can help to stabilize you if you are feeling fragile.

The color
of nature

Green relates
to the heart

Cautions

Green is probably one of the safest colors of the spectrum. It is best avoided, however, in situations where you need to be mentally on the ball or are required to react quickly to what is happening, since it is such a good relaxer.

Healing with Green

Treatment with green can benefit the following conditions:

PHYSICAL CONDITIONS

heart problems

bronchitis

flu

claustrophobia

NEGATIVE STATES OF MIND

instability

brooding

fear of emotional involvement

spite

A matter of balance

Green is in the middle of the color spectrum and holds the balance between the red (hot) and blue (cold) ends. If you are lacking in green energy, you are likely to be off center. To be "green with envy" or jealous is to be emotionally out of balance, to harbor feelings of bitterness or resentment, hostility, or even hate.

Using the Color Green

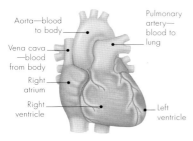

Aorta—blood to body
Pulmonary artery—blood to lung
Vena cava —blood from body
Right atrium
Right ventricle
Left ventricle

Heart
*Just as green is the central color
of the spectrum, so the heart is the
central organ of the body.*

The part of the body that the color green relates to is the heart, the muscular organ that pumps the lifeblood through our bodies. The heart is also the seat of the emotions, especially love, the most powerful emotion of all. The importance of this organ is reflected in the many sayings in which the word "heart" appears.

If we "break someone's heart," we cause someone deep emotional pain; when we "lose heart" or say we "haven't the heart" for something, we mean that we have no desire to do it, we cannot motivate ourselves. Similarly, when we speak "from the bottom of our hearts," what we say is sincere, driven by profound emotion.

When two people have a "heart to heart," they open up their hearts to each other—they hold nothing back, the emotions flow freely. Likewise, when we do something "whole-heartedly," we give it everything we have got. Someone with a "heart of gold" is a generous person, who will help someone else without thought of reward. In contrast, someone with a "heart of stone" is cold, unfeeling, and unlikely to answer a plea for help.

Heart attacks

It is generally accepted that heart attacks can often be caused by a deep-seated emotional problem, sometimes to do with a relationship. They may be brought on by repressing emotions, fear of emotional commitment, or by being stuck in life and unable to change. Many men have heart attacks in middle

"I am open to receiving everything that the universe has to give me."

age, which perhaps can be partly attributed to the fact that their heart is no longer in their career and gives out under the stress of the job.

Restorative power of green

One exercise you can do is to stand with your back against the trunk of a tree, then put your left arm out behind you around the tree, while holding your right hand over your solar plexus. Breathe in deeply, drawing the energy of the tree into yourself, then breathe out again. You will find that this will energize you and help to calm you down if you are feeling agitated.

Green Keywords

Positive open, grounded, sympathetic, compassionate, generous, relaxed

Negative envious, mean, bitter, inflexible, jaded

Delphinium
The blue flowers of the delphinium are relaxing on the eye.

BLUE

is the color of the sky and the sea; looking up at a cloudless blue sky or gazing out at the sea can often still the mind and soothe the spirit. It is no coincidence that when we want to "get away from it all," we often choose to take a vacation where we can gaze at limitless expanses of both sky and sea for hours on end, becoming so relaxed that we lose all sense of time passing.

By the sea
A vacation by the sea helps us unwind and forget our cares.

Blue is associated
with the throat

The color blue is
calming and
cooling

Blue benefits

If you have difficulty
sleeping, it can help to
visualize or breathe in
blue (see pages 134–137
and 146–147). Introducing
blue food into your diet can
help alleviate a "red"
condition, like a headache,
that has been brought on by
stress. Blue
is also noted for its
astringent and antiseptic
properties, and it is
therefore suitable for
treating infections or
inflammations.

Blue is the first of the cool
colors of the spectrum and
its action is opposite to that
of red. Where red
stimulates, expands,
and warms, blue calms,
contracts, and cools.

Cautions

If you are feeling low or cold,
or there is tightness
or stiffness in your body, you
should avoid this color.

Healing with Blue

Treatment with blue can benefit
the following conditions:

PHYSICAL CONDITIONS

high blood pressure

laryngitis

fever

cuts

stings and burns

menstrual problems

migraine

children's illnesses—measles,
mumps, teething

NEGATIVE STATES OF MIND

timidity

frigidity

fear of speaking
out/confrontation

distrust

Using the Color Blue

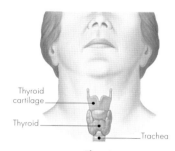

Throat
*Blue is associated with
the throat and the power
of speech, also wisdom.*

The thyroid gland, which is the
organ situated in the front of the
neck connected to the larynx, is
associated with the color blue. The
chief function of this gland is to produce
the hormone controlling the body's rate
of metabolism. It is one of the most
important hormones in the human body;
if it is deficient in children, they fail to
grow and if it is deficient in adults, they
become obese. Blue also governs the
throat, which is the center of speech,
communication, and self-expression.

The color is associated with intelligence
and the ability to speak your mind as
well as to conciliate, or make peace,
with words. Honesty and integrity are
also "blue" qualities; when we describe
someone as "true-blue," we mean we
can count on them because they are
loyal and trustworthy.

Speaking out

If you find it difficult to speak out, or
cannot find your voice, it can help to
treat yourself with blue. This may well
clear the blockage, whether physical—
in the form of a sore throat or
hoarseness—or psychological, in the
form of a terror of public speaking. Just
wearing a blue scarf around your neck
can help you overcome your fear.
Singing in the shower can also do the
same thing so it's a good place to
practice using your voice.

With blue, the focus of our attention
begins to shift inward, away from the
physical world and toward the spiritual.
It is the color of contemplation and quiet
reflection and a blue lamp or candle

Blue Affirmation

"I am at peace with myself and the world."

can be an aid to meditation (see pages 108–109). This will slow down the mind so that thoughts of a more inspirational nature may enter. Blue is also associated with writers, poets, and philosophers.

Unfortunately, the "blue" facility with words does have its negative side. The persuasiveness of "blue" people, who are able to cajole you into doing what they want almost without your realizing it, can easily turn into manipulation. Similarly, in an attempt to avoid quarrels and confrontation, "blue" people may unwittingly provoke dissent and argument.

Blue Keywords

Positive introspective, contemplative, serene, fluent, tactful, sincere, faithful

Negative tongue-tied, manipulative, disloyal, withdrawn, cold

Iris
The deep blue color of indigo, as seen in the iris flower, helps free the imagination.

INDIGO
Indigo is the color of the sky at night—a deep, dark, velvety blue, both mysterious and unfathomable. When we gaze at it, our thoughts are likely to turn inward, causing us to ponder on the deeper meaning of life. At such times we are likely to have flashes of insight that do not come to us during the bright, busy, daylight hours.

The fortune-teller
The fortune-teller is inspired by the intuitive color of indigo to give insights into the future.

Indigo is
associated with
the brow chakra

Indigo relates
to intuition

Psychic power

Indigo purifies the
mind, as well as the
blood. It frees us of
the fears and anxieties
that inhibit us to allow us
to hear our inner voice,
which knows what is best
for us. If you want to
develop your psychic
potential, it is a good
idea to treat yourself with
indigo, visualizing the color
or meditating on it (see
pages 140–141 and
146–147). It will lift you onto
a higher plane to enable you to
see with the inner eye. The
insights of indigo can also
help with deciphering the
meaning of dreams.

Like all the colors at the blue
end of the spectrum, indigo
helps to take us away from the
world of the mundane, to more
spiritual dimensions, where
intuition is more important
than reason and faith more
important than proof.

Cautions

If you are suffering from mental
illness or SAD, Seasonal
Affective Disorder (see pages
24–25), or are disturbed by
paranormal phenomena, you
should avoid indigo; it will only
exacerbate the condition.

Healing with Indigo

Treatment with indigo can
benefit the following conditions:

PHYSICAL CONDITIONS

deafness

cataract

hemorrhage

nerves

NEGATIVE STATES OF MIND

obsession

paranoia

hysteria

oversensitivity

Using the Color Indigo

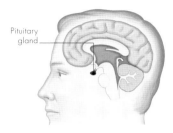

Pituitary gland

Master gland
The color indigo is associated with the master gland of the body, which produces important hormones.

Indigo relates to the pituitary gland, which is situated at the base of the brain and is the most important endocrine gland in the body. It exerts overall control over other glands, including the thyroid and adrenal, through hormones it produces.

The color indigo and the pituitary gland are associated in particular with the brow chakra, which is located between the eyebrows in the center of the forehead. This area is perhaps better known as the third eye (see pages 36–37). This is the eye that sees what is invisible to the naked eye, far beyond the boundaries of time and space to other dimensions and realities. It is also known as the inner eye. When we talk of someone having "the sight," we mean that they have this psychic or clairvoyant ability.

Inspiration

Someone with this ability can tap into a source of inspiration that gives people on this ray a reputation as spiritual teachers and healers. Going to a class or a talk given by such a person can act as a form of indigo treatment, helping to heal deep emotional hurts that have perhaps not been dealt with since childhood.

There are many such people around today, especially because humanity is evolving toward the blue end of the color spectrum. More and more people report being able to see auras (colored layers of light that emanate from the body—see pages 96–97), for example, or having dreams or visions that reveal their life path to them.

Indigo Affirmation

"I trust my intuition to guide me on my path through life."

Helping others

Frequently such people develop the gifts of healing or psychic sensitivity, in order to be of service to their fellow human beings. It is as if the third eye of humanity is collectively being opened at this time in history and we are all discovering that we have something to offer others.

However, on the negative side, "indigo" people can become completely fanatical about things in which they believe, driven by a reforming zeal that is deaf to other people's points of view. This kind of blind devotion or prejudice can lead to intolerance and create division.

Indigo Keywords

Positive psychic, deep, visionary, wise, inspired

Negative fearful, arrogant, deluded, isolated, overidealistic

Glorious purple
The glorious purple of the violet helps take our mind away from everyday concerns.

VIOLET

The violet is a small and humble flower, yet to look upon a clump of them uplifts the spirits, and its sweet scent delights the senses. There is something noble about violet or purple and these colors have traditionally been worn by kings, clergy, and those of high rank. In fact, at one time it was forbidden for lowlier folk to wear them.

Inspiration
In violet the blue colors of the spectrum reach their highest expression and this color is associated with sacrifice, whether to a cause, ideal, or to art. Violet is the color of transcendence, of mind over matter and the higher self over the lower self. It is the color of the divine inspiration, which is channeled by healer and artist alike.

Noble purple
Throughout history violet or purple has been worn by royalty and senior clergy.

Violet contains
balancing
energies

Violet is an
inspirational color

Violet is a color to be avoided
by people who suffer from
serious mental disorders or
those who have problems with
alcohol or drugs.

Meditative color

If you are generally
lacking in inspiration,
or you feel your life lacks
meaning, then violet is a
good color to meditate
on (see pages 140–143),
since it helps to develop the
psychic or creative faculties.
Meditating on this color may
also help you contact your
spirit guides, to obtain help
in finding the right direction
for your life.

If you feel like retreating
from the world, or just want
to take things quietly, it can
help to switch to a diet
containing violet or purple
food, as this will calm
you down and nourish
the spirit.

Healing with Violet

Treatment with violet can benefit
the following conditions:

PHYSICAL CONDITIONS

concussion

epilepsy

neuralgia

multiple sclerosis

NEGATIVE STATES OF MIND

neurosis

loss of faith

despair

lack of self-respect

Using the Color Violet

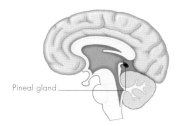

Pineal gland

Right brain
*The color violet is associated with
the right side of the brain, the site of
intuition, inner vision, and clairvoyance.*

Violet is a good color for those of an
artistic or highly strung temperament;
such people tend to be naturally in tune
with the color's vibration. It also helps
to soothe frayed nerves and bring
peace to troubled minds. If you are
feeling the strain of a modern, busy
lifestyle, treatment with this color can
help to restore your sense of balance.

Masculine and feminine

Violet consists of both blue and red
and, because of this, it helps to
balance both ends of the color
spectrum. The warm colors are
associated with the masculine energy
and the cool with the feminine, so violet
can help to bring these two energies
into balance within a person.

Violet is the color of the pineal
gland, so-called because it is
shaped like a pine cone. It is a
pea-sized organ that is situated in the
brain and it secretes melatonin and
serotonin, the hormones that regulate our
biological clock (see pages 24–25).

Violet vibrates at the highest
frequency of all the colors of the
spectrum and so it stimulates the highest
expression of the human spirit. It is the
color of the mystic and, together with
indigo, aids in the development of
clairvoyance and psychic sensitivity.

The overall effect of violet is to unify
body and mind with spirit, the
demands of the mundane world with
the need to feed the soul, and the inner
with the outer. People who manage to
achieve this unity know a peace that
escapes many in our modern,
materialistic society.

Violet Affirmation

"I seek to become whole in order that I may better serve."

"Violet" people are also likely to know why they are here, and will have a sense of destiny, which often involves dedicating themselves in some way in the service of humanity. They make powerful and effective healers; if they are artists, their work speaks to the nature of the human condition in a way that all may understand.

However, violet has its negative expression and this takes the form of overweening pride and a sense of superiority. The power of this ray will backfire if it is not used wisely, in the service of others rather than to further your own ends.

Violet Keywords

Positive spiritual, noble, dignified, inspired, humble

Negative fanatical, perfectionist, self-doubting, self-destructive, alienated

Turquoise
The turquoise stone contains copper and is a good conductor of healing.

TURQUOISE
While not one of the seven rays, turquoise is an important healing color. To many civilizations and peoples—the Atlanteans, Egyptians, and Native Americans—both the color and the stone were sacred and were worn for protection. Turquoise was thought to symbolize the heavens; the spirit as opposed to the flesh. Turquoise is a mix of blue and green, the colors of the sea, and it combines the qualities of both—the serenity of blue with the harmony of green.

The sky
To Native Americans the color turquoise symbolized the sky and the breath of life.

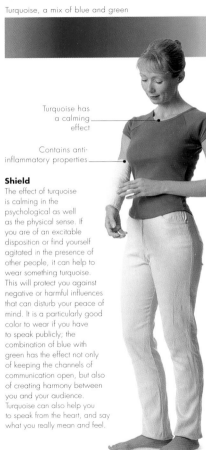

Turquoise has
a calming
effect

Contains anti-
inflammatory properties

Shield

The effect of turquoise
is calming in the
psychological as well
as the physical sense. If
you are of an excitable
disposition or find yourself
agitated in the presence of
other people, it can help to
wear something turquoise.
This will protect you against
negative or harmful influences
that can disturb your peace of
mind. It is a particularly good
color to wear if you have
to speak publicly; the
combination of blue with
green has the effect not only
of keeping the channels of
communication open, but also
of creating harmony between
you and your audience.
Turquoise can also help you
to speak from the heart, and say
what you really mean and feel.

Healer

Like blue, turquoise has anti-
inflammatory properties, and
is a good color to visualize
(see pages 146–147) for
a cut or burn because it
helps to soothe and heal
the wound. Turquoise is
also known to help boost
the immune system and it
is a good color to treat yourself
with if you are suffering from a
cold or the flu.

Turquoise Keywords

Positive composed, clear,
creative

Negative vain, boastful,
confused

Turquoise Affirmation

"I express what I think and feel
with clarity and conviction."

SECRETS OF COLOR HEALING

67

Primary and Secondary Colors

White light
If you project the colors red, green, and blue on to the same spot, you will get white light.

Primary colors are so-called because all the other colors can be produced by using a mixture of them. However the definition of primary colors differs according to their source.

Color in light

If the source is light, then the three primary colors are red, green, and blue-violet, known as the additive colors, which, as Sir Isaac Newton discovered, combine to produce white light. If you direct three spotlights of these colors onto a white screen or wall, at the point where they overlap, you will see white light. When you combine two of these primary colors, you produce the secondary colors yellow, from red and green, cyan or turquoise from green and blue, and magenta from red and blue-violet.

Color in nature

So far only the color of light has been discussed, but there is also pigment color, which occurs, for instance, as chlorophyll in green plants and hemoglobin in red blood. Pigment has come to mean any substance that imparts color and can be used to stain fabric, skin, or hair, such as a dye.

There have always been natural dyes, such as indigo, woad, and alizarin, which can be obtained from various plants, but the huge range of synthetic dyes available today dates from the middle of the last century.

Pigments and dyes

In the case of pigments or dyes, the primary colors are different to those of light. They are red, yellow, and blue, and these are known as the subtractive colors.

If you mix the colors red, yellow, and blue together, you produce black, because these colors absorb light. When you mix two of them together, you produce the secondary colors of orange (red mixed with yellow), green (yellow mixed with blue), and violet (red mixed with blue).

In addition to red, yellow, and blue, the human eye also discerns green as a primary color. If combined, these four colors produce a silver-gray.

The First Synthetic Dye

In 1856, an Englishman, William Perkin, succeeded in making the first aniline dye from coal tar. This was mauve in color and quickly led to the commercial production of hundreds of different colored dyes.

Fuchsia
The vivid magenta flowers of the fuchsia plant are a voluptuous sight.

MAGENTA
This is a deep purplish red color, made up of a combination of red and violet, and it is named after a town in Italy where a particularly bloody battle was fought in the mid-nineteenth century. It is also known as a brilliant crimson dye, sometimes referred to as fuchsin or fuchsine after the fuchsia flower. In modern times a bright magenta has been called a "shocking" or a "hot" pink.

Battle
The bright crimson of magenta is the color of blood shed in battle.

A new start
If magenta starts appearing in your life, perhaps in the form of a new desire to wear the color, you are now ready to let go of old habits or patterns in order to make way for the new. Magenta signifies change, the releasing of what we have outgrown in order to move on. Introducing magenta into your environment will help you to make changes, even if you just do something as simple as putting a fuchsia plant in your surroundings.

On the physical level magenta helps to energize the adrenal glands and the kidneys and it can also act as a diuretic. Its energy is calming and soothing and helps to stabilize people who are emotionally volatile or likely to be aggressive or violent.

Strength and spirituality

The power of magenta derives from the strength of red and the spirituality of violet.

A transitional color

Lying as it does between violet at one end of the color spectrum and red at the other, magenta combines the qualities of both—the will and the authority of red with the spiritual power of violet. It is also the color of transition, the place where we find ourselves between the ending of one cycle and the beginning of another.

Magenta Keywords

Positive open to change, mature, organized

Negative superior, self-righteous, insecure

Magenta Affirmation

"I have faith that everything will turn out for the best."

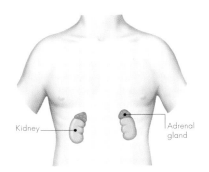

Kidney

Adrenal gland

Kidneys

The kidneys filter waste products from the blood, which are excreted as urine.

Tints and Shades

Blue and pink
It is traditional to give blue for a baby boy, and pink for a baby girl.

There are many subtle gradations of color, which vary in tone from light to dark, bright to dull. Those with a proportion of white in them are called tints; those with a proportion of black, shades. Pale colors have more white in them, while dark colors contain more black.

We tend to wear paler colors in the summer, because they reflect the heat and are cooler, while darker colors are better in the winter because they absorb the heat and are warmer. The colors we wear also reflect our mood or convey the impression we want to make. We choose bright, vibrant colors for leisure, and sportswear, when we want to relax and have fun, while somber colors are for more formal occasions, when we may have to keep our feelings in reserve.

Pink for a girl

All the colors of the spectrum have important tints and shades, with the exception of indigo, which does not have a tint. When we add white to red, for instance, we get pink, a soft and gentle color associated with the feminine and unconditional love. Although we now dress children in a whole range of colors, it is still customary, when a little girl is born, to give her something pink.

Blue for a boy

Blue, at the other end of the spectrum, is for boys; the pale blue that mothers have traditionally dressed their little boys in is associated with the more spiritual and peace-loving aspects of the color. The pastel colors of traditional babywear are protective, cocooning the child from too much stimulation too soon. Perhaps one of the reasons that children are growing up so quickly these days is that they are wearing much stronger and brighter colors at an earlier age than they used to.

Adding black to color

When we add black to red, we get the darker, sludgy shades of red, associated with the more negative qualities of the color, such as ruthlessness and brutality. Similarly, dark blue can denote a person who thinks he is always right, the dogmatist with set ideas. Generally speaking, the tints of a color are positive, while the shades are more negative.

Colors in Tints and Shades

Tints are colors containing a proportion of white, such as peach, apricot, lemon, primrose, pink, and light blue.

Shades are colors containing a proportion of black, such as dark blue and dark red.

Balance

This ancient Eastern yin/yang symbol represents balance between black and white, male and female.

BLACK is not, strictly speaking, a color, because it absorbs light, but it is important because it is the opposite of white. Without darkness, there would be no light. However, there is in fact a pigment, melanin, from the Greek word *melas*, meaning black, which ranges from dark brown to black. This is present at a higher level in the hair, skin, and eyes of black people and animals. Melanin is also responsible for tanning the skin and for melanomas, the tumors that occur when we overexpose our bodies to the sun.

Negative meanings

The word "black" tends to have negative connotations, such as in the "black sheep" of the family, the child who lets the other members down by behaving in a way that does not conform to their expectations. Then there are the "black arts" or "black magic," which involve invoking dark powers for evil ends. There is a seemingly endless list of terms with the word "black" in them that have only bad meanings.

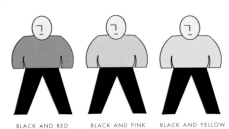

BLACK AND RED   BLACK AND PINK   BLACK AND YELLOW

Positive

There is a positive side to black. To be "in the black" with your bank account is better than being in the red! It is also one of the colors of the fertile earth and is associated with the Dark Moon, a very pregnant time. A seed planted then may grow to fruition at the Full Moon.

Black with other colors

Much of the superstition surrounding black is to do with its association with death, and also with power, which it lends to other colors when worn with them. Black with red denotes physical or sexual power; with pink, social status; and with yellow, mental superiority.

Melanin
The pigment melanin determines the color of the skin, hair, and eyes.

Black Keywords

Positive dramatic, dignified, discreet

Negative control freak, depressed, unapproachable

Black Affirmation

"I am in control of my life and no one can harm me."

Wearing Black

In control

Black clothes give the impression of being in control and remaining aloof from others.

Black has always had a place in the wardrobes of both men and women; it is the color of mourning, of formal business suits, and a favorite for glamorous evening wear. It has also become highly fashionable among the young, who dress in it from top to toe.

To wear black is to make a strong statement to others. When we don black for a funeral, we express sorrow for someone we have lost; when we wear a black suit to a business meeting, we tell our colleagues that we are in charge; and when we wear black in the evening, we say that we are alluring and mysterious.

Black confers dignity and power; the person who habitually wears black may seek to control others by keeping them at a distance, withholding information from them so that they do not gain either a psychological or a tactical advantage.

While the "black" person may well stay "on top," he or she may also have few close friends. Black has the effect of putting up a barrier between ourselves and other people, shutting them out, and ultimately this can lead to feelings of isolation and even depression. To counter its negative effect, black should be worn with a splash of color, perhaps by adding a tie, scarf, belt, or shawl.

A protective color

Black can also be protective and is a good color to wear if you are feeling vulnerable and need to withdraw from the world for a while. Perhaps this is why it is such a popular color with young people. The teenage boy or girl who will wear nothing but black is, after all, on the brink of a major threshold, from childhood to adulthood, which is one of the most difficult of transitions he or she has to make.

At this moment in history we are in the process of crossing over from one age to the next, which is the Age of Aquarius or the so-called New Age, with its increased emphasis on spirituality, holism, and the environment. We are experiencing a high level of collective angst as we embark on a new millennium, not knowing what it will bring. This may well have something to do with the perennial popularity of black as a fashionable color.

Goths

The epitome of worship of the color black among the young was perhaps the "Goth" fashion of the 1980s. Black velvet and leather featured strongly, together with jet black hair backcombed and hairsprayed into electric-shocked shapes to frame pancaked-white skin and dramatic eye makeup. This was a look that was worn equally by boys and girls.

Purity
The white of the bridal gown symbolizes virginal purity and innocence.

WHITE

The pure white flowers of the snowdrop are a sign of hope on a dark winter day that spring is on its way. We tend to respond positively to white because it contains all the colors of the spectrum and reflects light. It is the color of the bridal gown, a priest's vestments, and the crests of the waves that are sometimes called white horses.

Positive meanings
In contrast to black, most common sayings with the word "white" in them have positive meanings. A "white lie" is usually told in order not to hurt someone's feelings and "white magic," unlike black magic, is beneficent in purpose. To be "whiter than white" is to be as pure as the driven snow, without a stain on your moral character.

White horses
We associate the white horses of a choppy sea with the tang of salt and a fresh wind.

Spiritual

White is also associated with spirituality. Psychics and healers use white light to channel healing to those in need and you can meditate on it (see pages 140–143) to cleanse your system and give it a general boost. Many people who have come close to death as a result of illness or an accident in what are called near-death experiences, report being dazzled by white light.

White Keywords

Positive pure, innocent, orderly

Negative barren, critical, colorless

White Affirmation

"I have as much space as I need."

The status of a white coat

Many health professionals wear white coats, and while in this context white conveys an impression of cleanliness, it can also suggest superiority. This can make others feel inadequate or ill at ease.

Living with White

White room

A white living room may look light and spacious, but its starkness may not be conducive to relaxation.

White can be a difficult color to live with. While a room decorated all in white may be striking in effect, it does not make the most comfortable of environments. White can be stark and unrelenting and needs to be offset by touches of color in order for us to feel that we can relax.

Kitchens

A kitchen painted in white, for instance, may be light, cool, and airy, but can also look very clinical; not the sort of room in which you feel like chatting over a cup of coffee with a friend. It needs to be balanced by colored tiles or blinds, bowls of fruit and vegetables, or jars of warm-hued spices and legumes.

Bathrooms

Similarly, a white bathroom can look and feel cold, not the kind of room where you want to take off your clothes, let alone soak in a long, hot bath.

While white walls can reflect sunlight, many modern bathrooms are squeezed into small, windowless spaces and the monotony of the white needs to be offset by brightly colored tiles or towels, or a plant that will thrive in the humid conditions of a bathroom.

Bedrooms

White is also a popular color for bedrooms because it is clean and refreshing. An over-emphasis on the color, however, especially if your tastes are traditional and you like lots of crisp, starched white bedlinen or lace, can lead to the opposite of the effect you are trying to achieve. Instead of a room where you can take sanctuary from the hustle and bustle of everyday life, you may find that you have created a space that makes you feel lonely or cut off.

Try painting your bedroom in one of the shades of white, or off-white, that are now widely available. For example, a hint of peach or apricot will bring warmth to the room, while a blush of pink will aid rest. Curtains and pictures in a contrasting color can also help to soften the effect of white, which, on its own, can be harsh and even alienating. Or you can experiment with lighting (see box below), which can be coordinated with soft furnishings.

Lighting Tricks

The starkness of an all-white room can be minimized by clever use of lighting. Use lamps to add soft pools of light, and choose shades in colors that cast a warm glow, such as russet, terra-cotta, gold, burgundy, raspberry, or candy pink. Look for lampshade materials that allow light through, rather than just funneling it out of the top and bottom of the shade.

Ashes
*Gray ashes are all that is
left of the fire that has died.*

GRAY
is a combination of black and white but is neither one nor the other, hence its reputation for neutrality and even dullness. It is the color of ashes and of lead as well as the hue of the sky on miserable days when it is raining and we don't know what to do with ourselves. At these times we may not be depressed, but we are not exactly buoyant either.

Negative meanings
A "gray cloud on the horizon" indicates that something is on the way that may cast a shadow over the present. It is often something that we may fear, because we do not know what its outcome will be. A "gray area" is something that we are uncertain about and we may therefore take a noncommittal stance on it.

Positive meanings
Lying as it does between two extremes, gray has positive as well as negative meanings. It is the color of intelligence, as in "gray matter" or brain tissue. "Graybeard" not only means old man, but often wise old man or sage, too.

Silvery gray

In silver, gray takes on an almost magical connotation; silver is the color we associate with the moon and the feminine. It is used to describe movies, as in "silver screen"—here, we cannot be sure of anything we see, what is real and what is illusion—we are in the realm of the imagination and may therefore create our own reality.

Leisure wear

Gray is also a popular color for leisure wear; the clothes we relax and feel comfortable in—tracksuits and sweatshirts—are often made in various shades of gray.

Grey Keywords

Positive safe, impartial, restful

Negative uninteresting, indecisive, dismal

Grey Affirmation

"I take the time to make up my mind about where I want to go."

Tint and Shade Qualities

Scarlet Pimpernel
The color scarlet is bright and bold, the color of he who dares, despite the consequences.

and tenacity, while scarlet is associated with boldness and courage. An example of the latter is the Scarlet Pimpernel, the English nobleman who smuggled aristocrats out of France during the French Revolution. However, the color is also associated with lust and sexual promiscuity, as summed up in the expression "scarlet woman."

G enerally speaking, the clear, bright, strong hues of a color signify its most positive qualities, while the darker shades denote its more negative attributes. The pastel tints tend to stand for the color at its highest expression.

Red

We have already looked at pink as a tint of red as well as the darker shades of red; in between are the vivid crimson and scarlet. Crimson stands for strength

Orange and yellow

Peach and apricot, being tints of orange, are both positive in meaning. They are warm colors that induce a sense of well-being so are good to wear if you have to communicate with people or need their cooperation. Darker shades of orange indicate self-gratification or underachievement.

The pale yellows, lemon and primrose, bring out the best qualities of yellow—a good mind, discerning judgment, and the ability to distinguish truth from falsehood. This is the color of the intellectual, the philosopher, the person who searches for meaning. Dark yellow, on the other hand, is associated with a suspicious mind, destructive criticism, and malice. This is the color of the person who likes to pick a fight or who may be vindictive.

Green

Bright emerald green is one of the most positive colors in the spectrum, suggesting an abundance of what we need and generosity with what we have. It is associated with giving and receiving freely, so that all may be in balance. Pale greens relate to qualities of the heart, like sympathy, kindness, and compassion. Again, these are given without thought of what might be gained in return. Dark greens, however, are indicative of the darker emotions— envy, bitterness, and possessiveness.

The Message of Tints

This checklist shows the key characteristics of these tints.

scarlet lust

peach good communication

lemon clear mind

emerald abundance

Tiger's eye
The brown and yellow of tiger's eye are the colors of the Earth.

BROWN

This color has a plethora of associations with the Earth—everything from soil to rocks and minerals, the bark of trees, autumn leaves, seeds, and nuts. In the human and animal world, too, it features strongly—it is a dominant color of skin, hair, and eyes. The tiger's-eye stone, with its rich coppery colors, has many of the qualities that we associate with brown. It has a steadying influence, which helps us to stay on the straight and narrow; it also helps us to concentrate our energies on the task in hand, rather than dissipating them in all directions.

Nostalgia
Perhaps because of its association with autumn, brown can be associated with melancholy and nostalgia, but these are natural feelings, which need to be valued for what they are. We cannot be bright and happy all the time, any more than we can have eternal spring.

Mother Earth

Brown is the color of Mother Earth, which nourishes and sustains us all in a never-ending cycle of birth and death, growth and decay. In spring we plant seed, in summer we harvest fruit, and in autumn the leaves on the trees wither to brown and fall to become mulch for the next cycle. At this time of year we might wander through the woods in a "brown study" or reverie, absorbed in our own thoughts.

Reliable

We tend to take brown for granted, because it is always there, like the furniture of our homes, solid and reassuring. But without it our lives would lack stability. It is one of the colors favored in business, because of its association with reliability and a practical, common-sense approach. Most of us have worn the color at one time or another, even if only in the form of a pair of shoes, or an accessory like a purse or watchstrap.

Grounding

Brown is a good color to wear if you are feeling unfocused and need to ground yourself; or if you feel at the mercy of outside influences and need to protect yourself. However wearing too much of this color can make you afraid to embrace change and anything new or unfamiliar.

Brown Keywords

Positive secure, enduring, industrious

Negative conservative, fearful, boring

Brown Affirmation

"I am secure in myself and have everything that I need."

Tint and Shade Wisdom

Devotion
Blue is the color of devotion, whether to God, art, or a worthy cause.

On pages 72–73 and 84–85 we examined the meanings given to some tints and shades. Now we take a look at the meanings of blue, indigo, and violet.

Blue

Pale blue is traditionally associated with baby boys; however, this particular blue is also blue at its most ethereal and it represents devotion to a high ideal. Deep blue, on the other hand, symbolizes the best of "blue" qualities: loyalty, integrity, and trustworthiness.

The darker shades of blue, like those of most colors, carry a negative connotation, with the exception of navy blue, which is so-called because of its association with naval uniforms. This color stands for authority and sober judgment, which may be one of the reasons it is so often chosen for formal business clothing.

Indigo has no tint, but black mixed with this color can, for instance, turn an inspired teacher into a cult leader who demands blind obedience from his followers. Similarly, a deep, dark purple is associated with the high-ranking official who has been corrupted by power and abuses his position.

The lighter purples like lavender, lilac, and amethyst bring out blue's more mystical, healing, and aesthetic properties, symbolizing the highest expression of which we are capable.

The hidden meaning of color

All colors, with the exception of the primary colors, are a made up of a mixture of other colors. Orange is made up of red and yellow, yellow consists of red and green, green is a combination of blue and yellow, and so on. It is important, when using colors for healing purposes, to be aware of the colors that go to make up a particular color, because the body will experience the vibrations coming from all these colors.

So if you are treating yourself with the color green, for example, you will not only experience the harmony of green itself, but also the calming influence of blue and the mental stimulation of yellow. This is what makes green such a good color for healing, because it balances both ends of the color spectrum.

Sensing Color

The primary way that we sense color is obviously through the eyes; however, we also sense it subconsciously through the skin.

It is possible to develop this sensitivity in order to identify colors by touching them with our hands. Indeed, many blind people are able to differentiate colors in this way.

Opposites attract
Opposites attract, whether the poles of a magnet or complementary colors.

COMPLEMENTARY COLORS Each

color has its complementary color, which lies opposite to it on the color wheel (see page 35). While green is the complementary color to red, for healing purposes it is blue that is used. A color and its complementary color balance and attract each other like poles of a magnet, which is a very important consideration in color healing.

"Seeing" the complementary color

Even without looking at the color wheel, you can see the complementary colors for yourself by doing a very simple exercise. Stare hard at a red object, for instance, for a few seconds and then look away to a sheet of white paper or a white wall. You will see the after-image appear on the white in the form of the complementary color, in this case green. This has its counterpoint in nature, in the second rainbow we can sometimes see in the sky. It appears above the first rainbow, but if you look closely at it, you will see that its colors are in reverse order, with the blue colors at the bottom of the arc and the red at the top.

Stare at colored object

After-image in complementary color

90

Rainbow

To see how the colors complement one another, you have only to look at the rainbow that appears in the sky after a storm, arcing over the land in a vivid display of color.

Complementary Colors			
red	green	blue	red
orange	indigo	indigo	orange
yellow	violet	violet	yellow

Mixed colors

It is a little harder to see the complementary colors in colors that have been mixed, such as with paint. If you are looking around a room at home and feel that the colors are out of balance, but are not sure what other colors to introduce, you can carry out the same simple test described on the previous page. Just stare at the wall or the sofa in the color that is disturbing you and then look away to a sheet of white paper. You will see its complementary color and this is what you need to match as nearly as possible in some way in the room, in order to co-ordinate your color scheme.

Generally speaking, the lighter the tint, the darker the shade that is required to complement it.

Complementary Colors in Healing

Stress
If you find yourself in a stressful situation, the color blue will help you keep your temper.

Any disease or disharmony within the body shows up as an imbalance of color energy. For example, if you are suffering from high blood pressure or are feeling angry or irritable, then there is an excess of red energy in your system. The appropriate color to treat yourself with is the complementary color, blue.

It may be that you are sitting in a traffic jam, fuming at the delay as you need to keep an important appointment. You obviously will not have access to colored lamps or filters

but you can meditate on blue (see pages 140–143), or even just look out of the window at the blue sky. You will find that your anger dissipates and you begin to calm down.

Likewise, you may go to a beauty salon for a relaxing massage and find that the treatment room is decorated in yellow. As even the pale tones of this color can be overstimulating, ask the therapist if he or she has a purple towel that can be put over you or, while you are lying there, visualize the color purple (see pages 146–147). You will soon find that the decor ceases to disturb you.

Treatment times

This principle of treatment with complementary colors is all-important in color healing and also extends to ensuring you treat the complementary color with its own complementary color at the end of a color healing session. For example, if you are receiving treatment with blue for, say, high blood pressure or stress—which are red conditions—then it will be necessary to have treatment with red in order to complete the session.

Many color therapists, particularly those using lamps or filters in their treatment, have exposure times to all the different colors worked out to the minute, or fraction of a minute. It is wise, if you are considering doing a treatment for yourself, to consult a qualified color healer first about how long to treat yourself with each color.

Green

If you are ever in doubt about the effects of a color, or feel you have exposed yourself for too long to a particular color, you can always treat yourself with green, or even just visualize it, to remedy the situation. Green, being a neutral color, will correct any imbalance you have inadvertently created.

METHODS OF COLOR HEALING

In this section of the book you will be introduced to methods of color healing that you can try out for yourself without going to any great expense or trouble. It may be that you are feeling dispirited or stressed, or are suffering from some kind of physical illness. Whatever it is, you are likely to be aware of an imbalance of energy within yourself that treatment by color can heal. Some of the methods that are described go back to ancient times, like color breathing or drinking colored water; others are more modern, involving the use of lamps or colored filters. However they are all relatively simple and easy to practice. Remember that color healing by itself is not necessarily going to put matters right and, if you have a serious health problem, it is important that you consult your doctor or another qualified health professional.

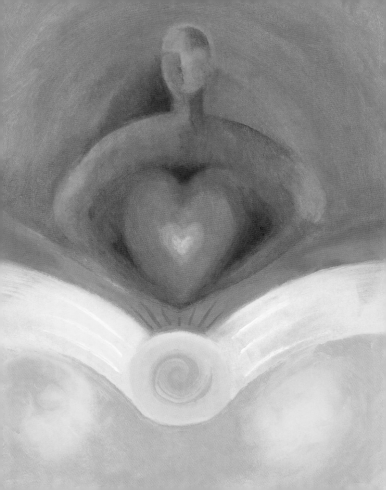

The Aura

Bands of color
The human body is surrounded by light or energy in bands of different colors, known as the aura.

An aura is the light or energy that emanates from the body of a human being or animal; it is actually also emitted by plants, stones, and any visible object.

An aura is usually described as being shaped like an egg, or an oval, and, in most people, it extends 2–3 inches (5–8 centimeters) around the body in different layers or bands, in different colors. The band nearest the body is called the etheric sheath, also known as the etheric double, because it is the counterpart of the physical body.

The etheric sheath draws vital life force from the atmosphere and distributes it through the chakras or energy centers (see pages 100–101) in the body.

Reading the aura

The aura says a great deal about a person's physical, mental, and emotional state, and spiritual development. The size and condition of the aura varies— the more highly evolved someone is, the larger and more radiant their aura is likely to be. Conversely, the aura of a person who is not well or whose energy levels are low, appears duller and smaller than normal.

In the early twentieth century, Dr. W.J. Kilner invented a device that came to be known as the Kilner screen. This was a kind of lens, consisting of two pieces of glass, between which a solution of an indigo-violet dye was poured, enabling Kilner and his colleagues to perceive the aura of their patients and to make their diagnosis accordingly. An excess of red might indicate stress, for example, for which treatment with blue was appropriate; an abundance of blue meant a lack of energy, for which treatment with red was appropriate.

Kirlian photography

In 1939 a Russian scientist, Semyon Kirlian, discovered how to photograph the energy field of humans and other living things, arousing interest in the aura as a means of diagnosis. He demonstrated that a photograph taken of a leaf just after it was picked, showed a bright, clear energy field, but one taken an hour later showed the field had diminished in size and color.

In recent years, Dr. Thelma Moss of the University of California, Los Angeles has shown that Kirlian photography can distinguish cancerous from normal tissue, but as a diagnostic tool it remains controversial.

The Weather Vane of the Soul

The famous American clairvoyant, Edgar Cayce, put it beautifully when he said that for him, "the aura is the weather vane of the soul. It shows which way the winds of destiny are blowing."

Shimmer
The aura of a candle is the faint shimmer around it.

HOW TO SEE AN AURA

Nowadays you can walk into a mind, body, and spirit festival, sit down in front of a computer, and have your aura photographed in seconds. However it is possible, with a little practice, even if you are not a natural psychic or sensitive, to train yourself to see the auras of other people with your own eyes.

Focusing on an aura
Most of us are familiar with the experience of looking at a lighted candle and after a few moments, seeing a faint, fuzzy shimmer all around it. This is the aura or corona of the candle. Part of being able to see auras is the ability to keep looking at something while remaining relaxed. The meditation techniques described on pages 140–145 will help you to do this. You can try this with someone you know. Focus on some part of their upper body, such as their mouth or their ears and then let your gaze relax. After a while you may begin to see a glow around their head and shoulders, and then their whole body. Eventually you may be able to see different colors emanating from different parts of their body.

The clues to health

Aura colors will vary according to the person's general state of health and how they are feeling at the time, but you will soon learn to interpret them. In the aura of someone who is ill or depressed, for instance, the colors are likely to be very dark or subdued; in the aura of someone who is angry, there is likely to be a lot of red; and in the aura of someone who is a healer or a counselor, for example, you may well see purple, which is the color of service to others.

Dark-green aura
This person may be feeling bitter, envious, or resentful.

Future vision

As we evolve collectively to a higher level of consciousness, more and more of us are likely to develop the ability to see auras.

Meditation brings rewards

Learn to be receptive

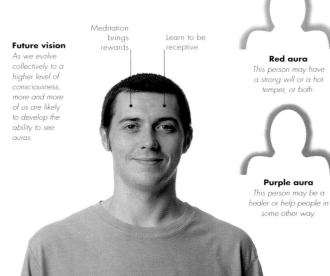

Red aura
This person may have a strong will or a hot temper, or both.

Purple aura
This person may be a healer or help people in some other way.

The Chakras

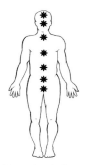

The major chakras
Five of the major chakras are aligned with the spine and they all relate to specific energies.

The different bands of the aura relate to the seven main chakras. "Chakra" is a Sanskrit word, meaning "wheel" and these energy centers spin clockwise or counter-clockwise, according to whether they are absorbing energy or releasing it.

Each chakra is located in a particular part of the body and is associated with a corresponding organ or gland. They are also related to particular properties: physical, emotional, and spiritual.

The seven energy centers

The root or base chakra is located at the base of the spine and is associated with the lower part of the body—the legs, feet, and intestines. It is also related to the reproductive organs. Our sense of reality, ability to fend for ourselves in the world, and overall vitality depend on this chakra.

The sacral chakra is located in the pelvic area, just below the navel, and is the body's sexual energy center. It is associated with the liver, pancreas, spleen, kidneys, and bladder, and as such, regulates bodily fluids. It is related to how well we feel.

Above the navel is the solar plexus chakra, which is associated with the stomach and the functioning of the sympathetic nervous system (this speeds up nerve responses). This chakra governs the passions, or "gut feelings" and it also influences our sense of personal power.

The heart chakra is situated in the center of the chest and relates to the thymus gland, which plays a vital role in the immune system. It regulates our emotional balance and rules love, compassion, and kindness.

The throat chakra is at the front of the throat and is connected to the thyroid gland, which controls the body's metabolism. It is the center of speech, communication, and self-expression.

The brow chakra, between the eyebrows in the center of the forehead, is associated with the pituitary gland, which controls the body's hormone production. This chakra is known as the third eye, because it sees clairvoyantly.

The crown chakra is on the top of the head. This is connected to the pineal gland, which influences the unconscious processes. The crown chakra is the center of spirituality or the soul.

Nadis

The chakras are linked by nadis, from another Sanskrit word, meaning "hollow stalk." Nadis are energy channels through which the prana, the breath of life, flows around the body. There are numerous nadis in the body, and they correspond to the acupuncture meridians.

Blocked energy
If someone is ill or feeling negative, the chakra colors will be weaker and dimmer, and energy flow blocked. Disharmony will show in the aura.

COLORS OF THE CHAKRAS
The etheric sheath, which surrounds the physical body, acts rather like a prism, refracting light into the colors of the spectrum, that then resonate with the chakras. The color of the base chakra is red; of the sacral chakra, orange; of the solar plexus chakra, yellow; of the heart chakra, green; of the throat chakra, blue; of the brow chakra, indigo; and of the crown chakra, violet.

Aura damage
The aura of a smoker or alcoholic will contain little specks of "dust," showing pollution to the system.

Bright, strong chakras

If a person's state of health is good and they are on an even keel emotionally, the colors will be bright and strong. They will also be in balance in relation to each other. The energy will flow from chakra to chakra, with no one color lacking or showing to excess.

Chakra Key

In descending order, according to their position in the body, the colors of the chakras are as follows:

- **Crown chakra** violet
- **Brow chakra** indigo
- **Throat chakra** blue
- **Heart chakra** green
- **Solar plexus chakra** yellow
- **Sacral chakra** orange
- **Base chakra** red

SECRETS OF COLOR HEALING

103

Blockages in the Chakras

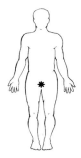

Base chakra

A blockage in the base chakra impairs the vital life force leading to feelings of exhaustion.

When our feelings are blocked and the flow of energy is restricted through the chakras, we do not function well either physically or psychologically. This manifests in different ways according to the chakra that is affected. The auras of people who are blocked in an emotional or psychological sense, perhaps as a result of feelings they cannot accept or let go of, will have gray in them; this might even actually show up as a knot or ball. In this context, gray is the color of fear and doubt; however, it is also the color of transition and indicates the possibility of change.

If the base chakra is affected, we may find that we lack the energy to do things, or we may suffer from chronic lower back pain. These physical problems, in turn, may be related to feelings of insecurity or being unsupported in the world. An excess of energy in this area could lead to violent, uncontrolled behavior.

If the sacral chakra is not functioning properly, both sexes may experience a variety of problems in the pelvic region, or may experience problems in sexual relationships.

Blockages in the solar plexus chakra may show up physically as ulcers or other stomach problems, indigestion, diabetes, or hepatitis. The psychological problems that may occur include stress or anxiety. Because the solar plexus chakra is related to our mentality, there may also be difficulty in thinking clearly or taking decisions.

Higher chakra problems

Any disturbance in the action of the
heart chakra is likely to result in heart
or lung problems. It may also cause
difficulties in relationships, because
a problem here inhibits the expression
of love. This in turn may be related to
a lack of self-love as well as a mistrust
of other people.

Blockages in the throat chakra tend
to manifest as thyroid problems,
laryngitis, or a sore throat. They can
also cause difficulty in voicing things
or speaking up for ourselves, or we
may be very opinionated and insist
that others share our views.

If the brow chakra is unstable,
we may suffer from insomnia, fatigue,
headaches, or nervous disorders.
We may also not trust our intuition or
capacity to perceive other realities.

Dysfunction of the crown chakra is
also associated with nervous disorders,
including multiple sclerosis. It is
also related to a lack of spiritual
awareness and a feeling that life
has little or no meaning.

Answer
Using a pendulum can help you find your own answer to a question.

DOWSING
If you feel that something is not quite right, either physically or emotionally, but are not sure what color you need to help rebalance your energies, then you can always try dowsing to find out which one you should use. To do this, you will need a pendulum, which you can easily make yourself.

Making and using a pendulum
To create a pendulum use a crystal that you feel particularly drawn to. Tie a piece of string or cord around it, making sure that there is enough slack to be able to dangle it. Then, unless you want to make your own color wheel, turn to the color wheel on page 35 because you will need it later.

Now you need to find out how the pendulum will work for you. Ask, out loud or in your mind, which way it is going to swing for a "yes" answer. After a second or two, the pendulum will begin to move, in a clockwise or counterclockwise direction, or from side to side. Do the same for a "no," and perhaps also for a "don't know, try again" answer.

Color wheel
This color wheel includes magenta, which lies between red and violet.

Color dowsing

Now you are ready to dowse for the color you need. First of all, be clear about the question you want to ask and frame it in such a way that the answer has to be a yes or a no. For example, you might be feeling a bit low, but not sure which of the warm colors you need. You could simply ask, "Do I need red/orange/yellow?" Then hold the pendulum over the color wheel and see in which direction it swings. It may be that it actually goes to the color you need. Then all you have to do is choose one of the methods of color healing described in the rest of this section.

Ask the question in your mind

Intuition

The beauty of this method is that you are using your own intuition and not relying on an expert or somebody else for the answer.

Hold pendulum over color wheel

Note the direction of the swing

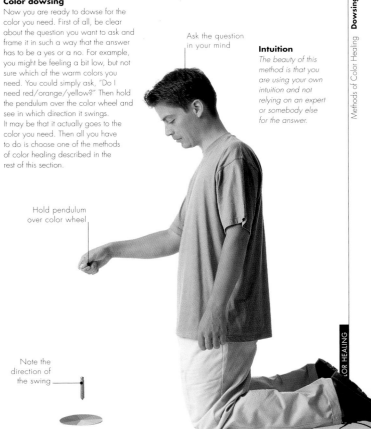

Healing with Colored Light

Atmosphere
Colored light is a very effective way of creating the atmosphere that you want in any room in the home.

Colored light healing is also known as chromatherapy, from the Greek word *khroma*, meaning light. This form of healing goes back to ancient times and the use of glass or crystals to filter the rays of the sun. Nowadays you can buy a variety of lamps for specific healing purposes. There is a lamp that will illuminate your surroundings with the color you require, whether it is blue for relaxation or orange for socializing, and so on.

However, without spending a lot of money, you can also create your own colored lamp by buying colored filters or gels from a specialist lighting or photography supplier. These can then be placed over an ordinary lamp at home, although care should be taken to leave a gap between the filter and the bulb, otherwise the filter will burn.

Alternatively you can buy colored light bulbs, which are widely available, and fit them to lamps that you already have. If your bedroom is a cold room, for example, fit an apricot- or peach-colored bulb in your bedside lamp, for a warm glow that will suffuse the room.

Candlelight

Another cheap but effective method is to burn a candle or tea light in a colored glass. If you are feeling stressed or harassed, for example, try placing a candle in a blue or indigo-colored glass; it will calm you down and it is also particularly good for meditation. Candlelight is soft and gentle and, when combined with colored glass, can help to induce a particular mood or feeling.

Treatment

Treatment with colored light usually takes two forms: it can be diffused over the whole body, especially the back, and this is generally used as a revitalizer; or it can be concentrated on one particular spot, where you feel out of balance or there is disease. If you are not sure what color to treat yourself with, try dowsing for it, or refer to the previous section of this book for lists of specific conditions and states of mind that are helped by treatment with a particular color.

The Nature of Light

Light travels through space in waves, at different frequencies according to the color. Violet radiates in short waves and pacifies, while red radiates in long waves and invigorates.

USING COLORED LIGHT

If you want to treat a specific part of your body with colored light, it is probably best to go to a trained color therapist, who will be able to ascertain what color you need and, most importantly, how long you should be exposed to it. Generally speaking, white or very light clothing should be worn during treatment, because this helps you to absorb the color better. If you wear a particular color, it may interfere with the treatment.

Light sources

There are specially manufactured light instruments, which are safe to use so long as you follow the instructions carefully. If, however, you just want to create a general effect of healing, then you can put a colored filter over a lamp or a colored light bulb in it, whether its a free-standing lamp, a bedside lamp, or an angle-poise lamp.

CANDLE

ANGLE-POISE
LAMP

BEDSIDE LAMP

Blue light calms and soothes away stress

Light is directed at a particular spot or diffused over a whole area

Light treatment

It can be dangerous to expose yourself to color for too long, particularly if it is at the red or hot end of the spectrum, otherwise you may end up creating an imbalance in your body. The treatment also needs to be completed with exposure to the complementary color for a shorter period. As a general rule, treatment with green and colors at the blue end of the spectrum should not exceed 15 minutes, while treatment with red should only be for less than half that time. Treatment with the complementary color varies between three minutes for red and blue and seven for green and magenta.

Exposure Time

If you are in any doubt about the time for which you should expose yourself to a particular color, a qualified color therapist will be able to help, particularly if you have a condition that would benefit from regular treatments.

Healing with Colored Water

Sun's rays
Water is energized by exposing a colored bottle filled with water to the rays of the sun.

This is one of the oldest methods of color healing and it is still practiced today in India by doctors of Ayurvedic medicine, as a way of introducing color into the body to alleviate its aches and pains. Quite simply, this method involves filling a colored container of some kind with water and placing it in the path of the sun, a process that is known as solarization. The sun's rays will then energize the water with the qualities of the color you have chosen. The ancient Egyptians made exquisite pottery jars of blue faience for this purpose.

The modern equivalent of the Egyptian jar can be seen today in the bottles and jars, made out of glass or plastic, that are used to package water, fruit juice, and various other soft drinks. A lot of mineral or springwater, for instance, is sold in bottles of varying hues of blue and green. These colors are deliberately chosen by the manufacturers for their cooling and thirst-quenching properties: try drinking water from a clear glass or bottle and then from a blue or green glass or bottle. Many people find that water from the latter tastes colder and fresher.

Decanting other liquids

This principle applies to other liquids besides water. You can decant milk, medicine, oil, lotion, and so on into a container of the appropriate color to enhance its effect. You might, for example, pour milk into an orange glass for a tonic drink first thing in the morning; cough mixture into a green bottle to help relieve the symptoms of colds or flu; or lavender body lotion into a purple container to augment its soothing and relaxing properties. You can even apply this principle to storing beans, legumes, or other foodstuffs in appropriately colored jars.

Generally speaking, drinking water that has been solarized with the red ray has an energizing or warming effect; while the orange ray has a vitalizing effect; the yellow ray, a stimulating effect; the green ray, a balancing or stabilizing effect; and blue, indigo, or violet rays, a soothing effect.

The Sun God Ra

The priests of ancient Egypt placed bowls of fruit and vegetable juice in the sun to absorb the energy of the sun god, Ra. The bowls were also set with jewels of the same color as the fruit and vegetables to enhance the effect.

Sunrise
The sun rises on another day, bringing light, energy, and heat.

USING COLORED WATER

Drinking solarized water is one of the safest ways to absorb color into the system. Once you have decided on the color you need, all you have to do is to fill a glass, jug, or other container with water and expose it to direct sunlight through a filter of the relevant color. Leave it to absorb the light for at least an hour. The water will retain its efficacy for a couple of days if you keep it refrigerated. Use a bottle or jar with a screw-top lid.

Energizing
Water charged with colors from the red, or hot, end of the spectrum is best taken early in the day, since it has a stimulating effect and helps to get you going.

BLUE GLASS

RED GLASS

ORANGE GLASS

YELLOW GLASS

Making solarized water

To make solarized water it is best to use mineral water, or water that has been passed through a water filter. You can tape or clip the colored filter around the glass or, alternatively, use a colored glass or bottle. Then put it out in the sun, perhaps on a windowsill, to absorb the light through the color, so that the water becomes charged with it. You will need to let the glass or bottle stand for up to an hour in direct sunlight, and even longer if it is not a sunny day. The water will keep fresh in the refrigerator for two to three days and can then be taken as required.

One hour
One hour in the sun should be long enough to solarize water.

Taste
You will find that water that has been solarized with one of the colors from the blue end of the spectrum tastes different from water solarized with one of the colors from the red end of the spectrum, and stays fresher longer.

Calming
Green, blue, indigo, and violet solarized water is best taken later in the day, since it has a calming effect.

VIOLET GLASS

INDIGO GLASS

GREEN GLASS

Color Baths

Soaking in color

Soaking in a color bath is a particularly pleasant and relaxing form of color healing.

Another way of absorbing the energy of color is to take a color bath. This can take different forms—you can use dyes or food colorings to turn the water the color that you want. If you do not like the idea of this, you can add bath salts, flowers, flower essences, herbs, or essential oils to the water.

There are many different kinds of foam baths and bath gels, but most of these are synthetic and are sold for their scent alone. Some products contain essential oils, which are very beneficial because they are 100 percent natural.

They are not only absorbed through the skin, but the scent can be inhaled from the warm bathwater. If you add essential oils to a color bath yourself, remember that only a very few drops are needed. Read the instructions on the bottle and follow them carefully.

Fragrance with color

Oils can also be added to salts for different combinations to relieve stress, clear the mind, or just to help you to feel good about yourself. The combination of fragrance with color is especially healing, so if you find yourself drawn to a particular flower for its scent and the effect it has on you, you might wish to throw a few of its petals into your bath as well. Try throwing in a handful or two of pink rose petals to give you a sense of well-being. Or float some stems of freesia on the water; their heavenly scent gives rise to an uplifting feeling. Freesias come in many different colors, so you can choose the color according to the feeling that you want to induce.

Flower essences

Flower essences are made from flowers that have been energized by being placed in pure water and exposed to the direct light of the sun. They are then combined with alcohol to make a tincture. They are perhaps best known as the products sold as the Bach Flower Remedies. These are named after Dr. Edward Bach, the man whose research between the years 1928 and 1932 gave us this form of healing.

Bach divided his remedies into seven groups, each one associated with a different color, to alleviate various negative states of mind. These remedies, too, can be added to a color bath for the desired effect.

Edward Bach

Bach was working in the London Homeopathic Hospital after the First World War, when he observed that people's illnesses seemed to be related to their personality. Negative moods and attitudes appeared to have contributed to their diseases. Bach set about developing the remedies to address these negative states.

Flower petals
A few colored flower petals in a bath can enhance the effect.

TAKING A COLOR BATH
When you take a color bath, it is important not to run the water too hot, otherwise it interferes with the effect of the color energy you are using and, if you are adding an essential oil, could also cause that to evaporate. You can have the water temperature a bit higher for a red, orange, or yellow bath, but it should be lower for a green, blue, indigo, or violet bath. It is, in any case, not a good idea to run too hot a bath because it is bad for the heart. A moderate temperature, close to body temperature, is best.

Essential oils
If you are adding an essential oil to your bath, sprinkle a few drops of it over the water once you have run it; if you are adding bath salts, throw them in and make sure that they have dissolved before you step into the water. Then soak in the bath for a while, at least 10 or 15 minutes, to allow yourself to absorb the energy of the color that you are using.

Meditation

The bath is a very good place in which to meditate (see pages 140–141), so you can combine these two methods of color healing. It would also help to visualize the effect you are trying to achieve (see pages 146–149). Or you can try breathing in the color that you want to absorb (see pages 134–135). However, it is important to remain alert so that you do not drop off to sleep in the bath.

Bath salts

Pink bath salts will help you feel good about yourself and attract the warmth and love of others.

Warm end of spectrum

Temperature

Baths of colors at the red end of the spectrum will raise your temperature on a cold morning. Baths of colors at the blue end of the spectrum will cool you down on a hot day.

Cool end of spectrum

Blue, indigo, and violet

A blue bath will help you unwind after a busy day and put your mind at rest. An indigo bath will help you escape from the everyday world and meditate on higher things. And a violet bath will inspire you to new heights of idealism in your work and life. All of these baths are best taken later in the day, when we are more inclined to relax.

Different Kinds of Color Baths

Time of day
Different colors of bath are suited to different times of the day or night.

Baths of colors that lie at the warm end of the spectrum are best taken in the morning, since they have a stimulating effect that will energize you for the day. You need to be particularly careful with red, however, because it is such a strong energy. Nevertheless, a red or an orange bath is a good treatment to take on a cold winter morning, since it will get the circulation going and help ward off colds and chills.

If your thinking is fuzzy or you find yourself unable to make a decision, you might want to add some yellow bath salts or a few drops of rosemary oil, which corresponds to yellow's color frequency, to your bath to help stimulate and clear your mind. The yellow bath is definitely not one to take before you go to bed since it makes you very alert.

A green bath is a particularly appropriate one to take in the summer, when you will be in harmony with the green of nature. It is also good in the afternoon, when many of us tend to slow down after the bustle of the morning. Such a bath will refresh and relax you.

Evening baths
Baths of colors at the cool end of the spectrum are best taken in the evening since they have a sedative effect. Try adding some blue bath salts or a few drops of geranium essential oil to your bath, to help dissolve the stress and tensions of the day. Alternatively, several

drops of patchouli oil will help you to reflect on your problems and come up with intuitive solutions to them. Lavender oil is particularly good for adding to a bath taken just before you go to bed. It relaxes you both physically and emotionally and will therefore help you sleep. It is also an antidepressant.

Cleansing the aura

From time to time it is a good idea to take a bath to cleanse the aura. The aura collects negative energies from the environment and other people. Most of us will be familiar with the experience of feeling drained after being with certain people—this is particularly true for healers and other members of the helping professions.

A turquoise bath is especially good for cleansing the aura, as it strengthens the immune system; white bath salts are also good for this purpose. Even sprinkling some ordinary sea salt into your bath can help to renew your aura.

*The aura is the electromagnetic field
surrounding the body. Soma comes
from the Greek word for "body."
The hyphen connecting the
words indicates the relationship
between the two.*

AURA-SOMA

The name given to this particular form of color healing revealed itself to Vicky Wall, a pharmacist and chiropodist, while she was meditating one day in 1984. Since then, aura-soma color therapy has spread all over the world; thousands of people train to practice it and many more buy and use its products.

Balance bottles

Like other methods of color healing, aura-soma works on the principle of balance and its distinctive bottles of colored liquids are actually called "the balance bottles." The liquids come in two layers: the one on top consists of a mixture of oils and essences, while the one on the bottom is a solution of herbs. When shaken, the liquids combine into an emulsion that can be massaged into the skin. From there they are absorbed into the bloodstream and eventually by the organs of the body which, as we have seen, relate directly to the chakras (see pages 100–101).

Chakras

For each of the major chakras there is a corresponding balance bottle, whose colors will help its energy to flow and restore balance to that part of the body. There are many other balance bottles and combinations of colors designed to treat specific ailments or enhance certain qualities.

BASE
GOLD/RED

SACRAL
ORANGE/ORANGE

SOLAR PLEXUS
YELLOW/GOLD

HEART
BLUE/GREEN

THROAT
BLUE/BLUE

BROW
BLUE/PURPLE

CROWN
BLUE/PINK

Vicky Wall

Vision
*The colors for the balance
bottles came to Vicky Wall in
a vision one night.*

Vicky Wall was born the
proverbial seventh child of a
seventh child and from an early
age she had psychic and mystical
experiences. In her autobiography, *The
Miracle of Color Healing*, she tells the
story of how she was scorned by her
schoolfriends for remarking on the
colors of their auras and how, on
another occasion, she spontaneously
healed the aunt of a classmate.

It was not until much later in her life
that Vicky developed the mixture of
oils and essences that went into aura-

soma's beautiful colored bottles.
However, she saw her whole life as
a preparation for that moment. Born
into a Hassidic family in the early
years of the twentieth century, as a girl
Vicky was initiated into the healing
properties of plants by her father, a
master of the cabbala, the ancient
Jewish mystical doctrine.

When she was in her fifties, Vicky
suffered a major coronary, which was
followed some years later by a massive
hemorrhage that was to leave her blind
as well. However, true to character, she
regarded the consequent sharpening
of all her senses and, in particular, her
auric sight, or ability to see auras, as
compensation for this.

"Divide the waters"

Vicky had been making up healing
creams and lotions for years, but one
night while meditating she was told to
"divide the waters." She was mystified,
but the next night the injunction was
repeated. On the third night she got up
and with little sense of what she was

doing or how she did it, she made what came to be known as the balance bottles. These were of two layers of liquid, one lying upon the other, with the color on the top usually of a different color to the lower. The waters had indeed been divided.

Vicky was inspired to make many variations on her "colored jewels," as she called them, and today there are about one hundred balance oils. She also developed other ranges of plant essences and oils that she called pomanders and master quintessences. These differ from the balance oils in that they emit "fragrant vapors," although color is also the key to their healing properties.

The Balance Bottles

Each of the balance bottles has a name, such as "Peace," "New Beginning for Love," and so on, signifying its special quality. The different combinations of colors work on several levels—physical, mental, emotional, and spiritual. Their effect is subtle, rather than dramatic, and they help us relate to our true selves.

AURA-SOMA COLOR READING

The balance bottles work on many different levels—physical, emotional, mental, and spiritual. When you go for an aura-soma color reading, you will be asked to choose four bottles out of the whole range. You pick the ones you find yourself drawn to, using your intuition to guide you.

Choosing bottles

The first bottle represents your purpose in this incarnation, while the second shows the difficulties you have to overcome in order to achieve it. The third bottle stands for the here and now and shows how you are actually doing and the fourth reveals what the future has in store for you. Together they make up what Vicky Wall has called "a mirror of your soul."

Discussing your choice

You will then discuss the chosen bottles with the aura-soma color therapist, who will help you to relate the colors you have chosen to your physical and mental well-being, emotional state, and soul's evolution. At this point you will be asked to shake the bottles vigorously, so that the two layers of liquid are well mixed. While you are doing this you are also putting some of your own energy into the contents, increasing their healing potential.

Shaking the bottles

If you are in a generally healthy state, the bubbles produced should settle quite quickly; if you are not, the effect will be cloudy and this can take some time to clear. The therapist will then advise you on how best to use the bottles. The methods you will be told to employ are likely to include rubbing the shaken mixture into your skin, so that you can absorb the energy of the colors. You can also just place the bottles strategically around your home or office, so that you benefit from their healing qualities just by looking at them or having them near you.

Full personal picture revealed

Therapist reveals significance of colors

Crystals, Gems, and Stones

Ancient temples

In ancient times crystals were built into the very foundations of temples and other buildings.

Crystals, gems, and stones are formed from the minerals that make up the Earth's crust and part of their appeal for humanity is their timelessness. Throughout history they have never ceased to fascinate humans and they have been prized for the status they bestow, the luck they are thought to bring, and perhaps above all, for their special healing properties. Ancient temples were built out of them, Egyptian pharaohs were buried with them, and no modern state occasion would be complete without them. Crystals, gems, and stones are part of human myth and legend, and some of them have become legends in their own right, such as the famous Koh-i-noor diamond, which weighs 108.8 carats and literally means "mountain of light." The Koh-i-noor has a long and bloody history that goes back to the fourteenth century, but since the annexation of the Punjab in 1849 it has formed part of the British crown jewels.

Crystals

Crystals consist of millions of atoms and the density of these atoms is responsible for crystals' multifaceted shapes. When heat or pressure is applied to a quartz crystal, the atomic structure is disturbed, producing a current of electricity oscillating from one end to the other. This process is known as piezoelectricity and in modern times has been applied in radio, television, and satellite communications, as well as in technology requiring a high degree of precision. When the external application of pressure stops, the atoms rearrange themselves, so that the crystal is once more in balance. This shows, therefore, that crystals are both transmitters and receivers of energy, and it is thought that they can absorb and respond to our thoughts and emotions. They seem to have an ability to restore balance to a part of the body that is experiencing disease or disharmony. Crystals and gemstones have long been used for this purpose in India where, ground into a powder and mixed with water or simply immersed in liquid and placed in the sun, they are still prescribed by doctors of Ayurvedic medicine.

Koh-i-noor Diamond

The Koh-i-noor diamond resides in the UK as part of the crown of Queen Elizabeth the Queen Mother. The crown was created when she became Queen Consort in 1937. The diamond was originally presented to Queen Victoria in 1849 and worn by her as a brooch and circlet. On her death it became part of the crown jewels.

Right for you

Handling a crystal will help you decide if it is right for you.

CHOOSING A CRYSTAL
It is very important, when choosing a crystal for yourself, to follow your intuition and not to be swayed by what someone else thinks is right for you. Walking into a crystal shop or up to a stall selling crystals at an exhibition can be a bit mind-boggling at first, but if you focus on why you have come, you will find that a particular crystal will "speak" to you. It will pick you out of the crowd, as it were, and that is the crystal for you.

Handling your Crystal

Pick up the crystal you have chosen and hold it in the palm of your right hand (change this to the left one if you are left-handed) and see how it feels to you. Does it feel cool or warm? Does it make you tingle? You may not get any physical sensation at all, but still feel that it is right for you.

Many other people will probably have picked that crystal up and handled it before you chose it, so when you get home, you need to cleanse it of any negative energies that it may have absorbed. This can be done by taking a small bowl, preferably of glass or ceramic than of a synthetic material such as plastic, pouring some

mineral or filtered water into it and then adding some sea salt. Then place the crystal into the bowl and let it stay there for as long as feels right to you.

If the crystal is for your own personal use, do not let anyone else handle it. Place it in a sunny spot on a windowsill or the top of a bookcase. Crystals, being creatures of the Earth like ourselves, need sunlight and air, although sometimes it's appropriate to keep them wrapped up in a piece of dark-colored silk or other natural fabric to project them from negative influences. As you get to know your crystal, you will find out what it likes!

Ruby and garnet

The ancient Egyptians massaged themselves with rubies and garnets to stimulate the cells of the body. Both stones were also thought to bring luck and good fortune.

Peridot

In ancient civilizations this brilliant stone was used to purify both the mind and the body. It aids the digestion and is particularly good for cleansing the liver.

Amber and topaz

Both of these stones with their warm, golden hue will help to dissolve barriers in communicating with others when placed on the navel and solar plexus areas.

Amethyst

If you are a very emotional person, the amethyst will help you to stay in control. Placed between the eyebrows, it will also help activate the inner vision.

Quartz

The different kinds of quartz share the quality of breaking down negative patterns of behavior, clearing the mind, and generating positive energy.

Aquamarine

Associated with the sea, this stone is good for eliminating fluid from the body. It also helps with negative emotions, like anxiety and doubt.

Crystal Healing

Relax or work
Crystals can be placed around the home or office to help you either to relax or work.

Part of the healing power of crystals derives from their color. This is important to bear in mind when you find yourself attracted to a particular stone because it may be its color that is calling you.

If you find yourself drawn to one of the red stones—a garnet, carnelian, or agate, for example—it may be that you are in need of some red energy, perhaps because you are anemic or feeling listless, or your base chakra is not functioning well. The red stones motivate and energize us and are good for the circulation and sex drive. The king of the red stones, of course, is the ruby, which has the power to heal the spirit as well as the body.

Perhaps the best known of the orange stones is amber, the translucent fossil resin that sometimes contains trapped insects. Like its warm, glowing color, it promotes emotional well-being and gives protection against negativity from within yourself and from external influences. Another stone with similar qualities to amber is topaz, which is good for shock and emotional trauma.

The yellow quartz, citrine, stimulates the mind and helps communication with others. It is a good stone to have in your study if you are writing a report or an article that calls for clarity of thought. If it is placed in your office it will help you to make decisions.

Green, blue, indigo, and violet

Green is the color of the heart chakra and green stones can help with problems of the heart, whether physical or emotional. Wearing an emerald or a jade pendant over your heart will help you to open up to others, without any fear or inhibition.

The sapphire comes in many colors, but the blue variety is perhaps the most highly valued. It is associated with the "blue" attributes of truth, integrity, and wisdom. Aquamarine promotes tranquility and peace and it also soothes fever, stings, and burns. Its name comes from the Latin *aqua marina*, meaning seawater, and so it is also considered to bring luck to sailors and fishermen and to anyone making journeys by sea.

The stone that is most commonly associated with violet is amethyst. It has spiritually uplifting and transforming properties. Place one under your pillow at night to help you to sleep.

BioElectric Shield

The BioElectric Shield is a pendant containing quartz crystals, and is said to deflect harmful electromagnetic energy. Its famous devotees include Hillary Clinton and actors Bill Cosby and Steven Seagal.

Ancient
The ancients practiced color breathing as a form of color healing.

COLOR BREATHING

This is one of the oldest methods of color healing, which dates back to Atlantean times. It is also one of the simplest and cheapest as it doesn't involve any outlay at all. The key to it is the breath. This is what Hindus call *prana*, which is a Sanskrit word meaning "the life-giving breath."

Inhaling energy

Color breathing is literally what it says—breathing in color and then permeating the whole body with it, or directing it to a particular part of the body. One of the best times to practice it is at the beginning of the day—outside if possible if the weather allows and you have a patio, inside if you do not, preferably in front of an open window. You may well want to do one or two stretching exercises first, to limber up and relax your body.

Fresh air
If you can, do your color breathing outside, in the fresh air.

Breathe in
the color
and direct to
the chakra

Yellow
globe

Solar
plexus
chakra

How to color breathe

1 *Choose the color that you want to use—perhaps one of the warm colors to energize you for the day ahead.*

2 *Stand with your feet a little apart, arms stretched out to either side and eyes shut to help you focus.*

3 *Visualize a globe of the color in front of you, behind you and to either side of you. Now breathe it into the corresponding chakra. If yellow, for example, direct it to the solar plexus —hold it, and then breathe out again—this time without the color, because you have absorbed it.*

4 *Do the whole process again, circulating the color around the rest of your body.*

Color choice

You can use this method with any color or for each of the chakras, one after the other, if you like. If you choose one particular color, you may well find that you notice it more than usual during the rest of the day. Your environment, whether your home, office, or, nearby park, will reinforce it for you, in the clothes that people wear, the colors of flowers, and so on.

The Fourfold Breath

Practicing
Before you start practicing your breathing, make sure that you will not be disturbed.

Color breathing combines the act of breathing with concentration on a color. The energy of the color you inhale can be directed to heal a chakra that may have absorbed negativity from your thoughts and actions, and any part of the body.

If you are not accustomed to breathing in the way that is described on pages 134–135, you can practice doing it on its own at first, without the color, until you are used to it.

Breathing sequence

1 Choose a quiet moment and lie or sit down in a room on your own, making sure that you are comfortable.

2 Breathe in slowly and deeply for a count of four, hold for a count of two, and then breathe out again for a count of four.

3 When you breathe in, start right down in your belly, then let your diaphragm expand, and finally fill your lungs with air.

4 When you breathe out, reverse the process, letting the chest contract first, then the diaphragm, and finally the belly.

5 While you are getting the hang of this, it may help if you place your hand over your belly, so that you can feel it expanding and contracting.

Practice doing this until it feels natural to you, but be careful not to hyperventilate—most of us are shallow breathers and are not used to taking deep breaths. If you do find yourself feeling a little dizzy, just stop and breathe normally until you recover.

Environment

The beauty of color breathing is that you can do it anywhere, combining the color you breathe in with that in the environment. Try walking alongside a river or the sea, breathing in the color blue; not only will the water energize you, but when combined with the color blue, it will settle your mind, clearing it of mundane concerns and inspiring more spiritual thoughts.

Alternatively, as you walk over fields and through woods, breathe in the color green, which is the color of the grass beneath your feet and the leaves over your head. This will give you a deep feeling of harmony with your surroundings.

Affirmations

You can also practice your affirmations (see pages 40–41) as you walk; as you breathe in the color, say out loud (or silently in your mind if you prefer) the sentence that you have written for yourself. This will reinforce the positive attributes of the color for you.

Colors
Breathing in certain colors will help rid your aura of anything negative. Gold, blue, turquoise, and violet are the best colors to use for this.

THE CLEANSING BREATH
Just as you can take a color bath to cleanse your aura (see pages 120–121), you can also use the breath to cleanse it. Like anything else, the aura can get polluted by habits such as drinking and smoking, stress, negative environments, and negative people. The best colors to use to cleanse the aura are gold, blue, turquoise, violet, or, if you prefer, white light.

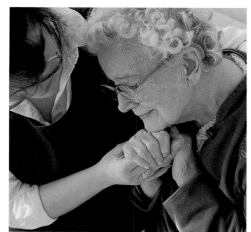

Helping people
If you help other people, then cleansing your aura should be part of your routine.

Bring blue, turquoise, and violet down from your crown

Bring gold through the soles of your feet

Cleansing the aura

1 Stand with your feet a little apart, with your arms hanging loosely by your sides.

2 Breathe in the color that you have chosen. If it is gold, bring it up from beneath the soles of your feet, up through the chakras, one by one; if it is one of the other colors, bring it down from just above the crown of your head, again through the chakras.

3 As you breathe out, without the color, imagine that you are expelling the tensions of the day, all the negative emotions, and anything else that your aura may have collected that you want to get rid of. If you have chosen the first method, you can imagine the waste disappearing into the ether; if the second, being buried in the Earth.

4 Repeat the process until you are satisfied your aura is cleansed.

Regular treatment

It is good to get into the habit of cleansing your aura regularly, particularly if you are a nurse or a therapist of some kind, as your work involves helping people who are ill or disturbed in some way. There are also people we meet in the course of everyday life who deplete our energy, leaving us feeling tired and low. If you feel this has happened to you, then just cleanse your aura in the way described, and then you can recharge it with one of the warmer, energetic colors.

Meditation

Peace and quiet
*It is important to have peace
and quiet if you are going
to meditate.*

Meditation involves going
within, to distance yourself
from the distractions of the
outer world and just to be with
yourself—or *your self*, that vital inner
part of you that it is so easy to lose
touch with in a busy life revolving
around home, work, family, and friends.

To do this, you need silence, which
many people in our busy, noisy modern
world are so unused to that they feel
unnerved by it. We are continually
bombarded by various levels of
background noise from things such as
radios, TVs, stereos, telephones, traffic

and so on. However, it is only when
the clamor of external life has been
tuned out that we can turn our attention
inward to reflect, dream, and meditate.

If you are not used to meditating,
don't worry as you will soon get the
hang of it. Like most things, it comes
with practice.

Meditation basics

The important thing, first of all, is to
make sure that you choose a time when
you know you will not be disturbed
by such things as the ringing of the
telephone, the doorbell, the demands
of children, or someone else walking
into the room.

One thing you will notice when you
start meditating is that your mind
chatters away about all kinds of
irrelevancies, such as what you are
having for dinner, or what so-and-so
said to you the other day. Just let these
things pass through your mind without
dwelling on them and you will find that
after a while, as your internal focus
grows, they fade into the background.

Meditating on color

Meditating on color is another age-old technique for self-healing. It allows you to focus on a particular chakra that may not be functioning well.

By meditating on the color associated with a chakra, you can restore it to balance and harmony. Say, for example, that you feel you are in a rut, that your life is going along all right, but you are bored and are not having a lot of fun. By meditating on the color orange you can regain your appetite for life, and this will help you to make the changes that will lead you to engage with it again. To find the best color to meditate on, refer to Colors of the Spectrum (see pages 22–93).

Meditation Benefits

Regular meditation can help improve a variety of conditions: headaches, migraines, anxiety, depression, asthma and breathing difficulties, insomnia, chronic pain, blood pressure problems, circulatory disorders, high blood pressure, stress-related disorders, and muscular aches and pains. It improves awareness, concentration, and emotional well-being.

Energy flow
Sitting with a straight back and feet on the floor will help the energy flow through the chakras. This pose is known as the Egyptian position.

MEDITATING ON THE CHAKRAS

Sit down in a chair, with your feet on the floor, your back against the back of the chair, and your hands resting on your thighs. This is known as the Egyptian position, after the pose of Egyptian pharaohs. Take a few moments to relax, making sure you are comfortable, before beginning your meditation.

Closing the chakras
It is very important to remember to close your chakras when you have finished your meditation. Otherwise you will be vulnerable to external influences. View your chakras like flowers, with the petals folding inward to protect the center. Then gently bring your awareness back to the present and, when you are ready, open your eyes.

Chakra meditation

1 Close your eyes—this will help you to shut out the external world and focus inwardly.

2 Start breathing in the way described on pages 136–137, and, after two or three fourfold breaths, let your breathing return to normal. As you breathe, open your chakras one by on. If you are not used to doing this, imagine that they are flowers, opening up to the light.

3 Now focus on the center of your chest, where the heart chakra is located. Imagine a ray of green light entering it from the side and filling it with love—for yourself, your loved ones, your neighbors, colleagues—even people that you do not particularly like or get along with.

4 Let the light radiate out through your upper chest, along your arms, and into your hands. Allow yourself to bask in the peace and harmony that it brings, as you are opening your heart to your fellow human beings, with whom you are one. This is a particularly good meditation to do if you are feeling lonely or have recently been hurt in a relationship.

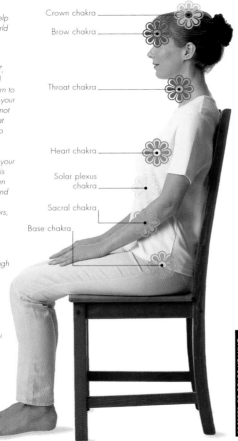

Crown chakra

Brow chakra

Throat chakra

Heart chakra

Solar plexus chakra

Sacral chakra

Base chakra

The Rainbow Meditation

Red, orange, and yellow
Bring in the red, orange, and yellow rays from beneath the soles of your feet.

The rainbow meditation is a wonderful way to start the day and you can combine it with color breathing. Take up position and relax as described previously. Now take some deep breaths and open up your chakras (see pages 136–137 and 142–143). Then imagine the red ray rising—or breathe it in—from beneath the soles of your feet up to your base chakra, allowing the color's energy and warmth to suffuse your whole body. (If you have heart trouble of any kind or you feel that red is too strong a color for you, you can use the pink ray instead.)

Next bring the orange ray up to your sacral chakra and feel a sense of joy and vitality pervade your whole being. It is a new day and you look forward to what it brings. Now turn your attention to the yellow ray, allowing it to rise from beneath the soles of your feet to your solar plexus and then to spread throughout your body. As it does so, feel your mind quicken and awaken to the possibility of new ideas.

Moving through the rainbow

Now it is the turn of the green ray; imagine it entering the heart chakra horizontally, and, as it does so, feel it bringing you a sense of peace and fellowship with others. As you circulate the color through your body, allow it to balance any part of you that feels out of kilter.

The blue, indigo, and violet rays should be brought in from just above the crown of your head. Blue then goes to

the throat chakra, first of all, to facilitate
fluency of speech and also the wisdom
to say what other people need to hear.
Imagine as your breathe it in that the
calmness of blue will stay with you
throughout the busy day to come.

Now imagine the indigo ray lighting
up your brow chakra, and as it does
so, it brings you insight into your life
and the intuition you need to navigate
the day successfully.

Finally, beam the violet ray down into
your crown chakra and feel its idealism
pervading your consciousness, inspiring
you to act for the highest good.

Remember to close your chakras
when you have finished this process.
You may also like to imagine yourself
wearing a cloak of white light to protect
yourself from negative energies
throughout the day.

Regular Meditation

If you do this kind of meditation regularly, you
may find that a particular color comes to you
as you prepare yourself. This is the one to take
in, since you may need it for the day ahead.

Techniques
Visualization uses the same relaxation and breathing techniques as meditation.

VISUALIZING COLOR

Here is a visualization that you might try for yourself sometime. First, take up position, relax, and start breathing as you did for color breathing and meditation. Next, open your chakras and then return your breathing to normal. Now, imagine that you are going for a walk through your favorite part of the countryside, and are leaving your everyday concerns behind. Already your heart feels lighter and there is a spring in your step.

The visualization
1 *You now take a path off the road, leading down to a meadow whose lush green brings you a sense of peace. Red poppies are dotted among the tall grass and the sight of them lifts your spirits. With renewed energy you go on your way.*

5 You make your way back to the spot where you joined the road, and begin to close down your chakras. In your own time bring yourself back to your real surroundings and open your eyes. You can do this visualization any time, anywhere—such as in the office.

4 A clump of harebells grows by your head. Idly you daydream. In this relaxed state, the answer to a problem that has been worrying you may come into your mind.

3 A little way off you spot a shady copse. You lie under a tree there, on ground dappled with warm, golden sunlight.

2 You reach a gurgling brook. Gazing into its clear depths, you feel the cobwebs lifting from your mind. You dip a hand in the water and its coolness refreshes you.

Visualization

Going to sleep
Before you go to sleep at night, train your mind to visualize the day's events and encounters.

Visualization is a similar process to meditation, except that it involves seeing or creating pictures with the inner eye, which is why it is sometimes known as creative visualization. This process comes more easily to some people than to others. Ask them what they had for lunch, and on to the inner screen of their mind will immediately flash a picture of a bowl of soup and a sandwich. You may be the type of person who senses things more, feels, or even hears them. However, with practice, even if you do not consider yourself to be a particularly visual person, you can train your mind to visualize, using your powers of observation and recall.

Bedtime

At night, before you go to sleep, go over the day, but instead of mulling over the problems that arose, think of the places that you went to or the people that you met and try and recall them in as much detail as possible. If you are recalling a person, then try to remember what they were wearing. How did they have their hair? And what were they carrying? If you practice this often enough, you are likely to find that you have only to think of a name for a picture to come to mind.

I spy with my little eye

Can you remember playing "I spy with my little eye" as a child, in the back of the car or on a train journey? Try it again the next time that you are traveling and have time to kill. Look out of the window at the landscape, at the buildings that are passing by, and note any special features that they have. Later on, try and recall what you have seen in as much detail as possible.

What you are doing with this process is training the mind to file away pictures for future use. Eventually you will get to the point where you will be able to summon up pictures from your mind's very own "picture library" at will, simply by recalling a name or a place. This is obviously a very useful ability to have if you go on the vacation of a lifetime and want to go back! All you have to do is file away the picture of the turquoise sea, the empty beach, or the mountain top and you can go back whenever you wish.

Mind Games

Visualization can be done any time and anywhere. That way, wherever you are and whatever the weather, you can always go to your own special place.

You can do it in the office during your lunch hour, perhaps using it to escape from a dark winter's day to a sun-drenched Mediterranean scene. Or you can visualize a favorite walk.

Your own needs

*You can combine different
color healing methods
to suit your own needs
and tastes.*

COMBINING METHODS

Visualization, meditation, and color breathing can all be enhanced by other methods of color healing, for example, crystal healing. A colored cloth is particularly useful if you have difficulty envisaging a color. Put it in front of you and look at it for a few moments. Then, the mental image will stay with you when you close your eyes.

Revitalizing

If you do decide to use colored cloth it is best to use pure silk or cotton, because they are natural fabrics and are therefore better conductors of the vibration of the color. If you have been working very hard and you feel physically run down and have difficulty motivating yourself, try meditating on the positive attributes of the color red—energy, will, enthusiasm—or visualize red going into your base chakra. It will help if you drape a piece of red cloth, such as a shawl or a scarf, over your pelvis. If you have a heart problem, of course, you should avoid using red. When in doubt, leave red out!

Visualize
red energy

Drape a red
cloth over pelvis

Raising self-esteem

ROSE QUARTZ

You can also use crystals in a similar way. If, for example, you are not feeling particularly good about yourself—perhaps you are estranged from someone or are not getting the recognition that you feel you deserve at work—then try using a piece of rose quartz to aid a meditation on the color pink. This is the color of love and it will help to raise your self-esteem as well as attract the love of others.

Relaxing

Alternatively, if perhaps you are in an agitated state of mind and cannot settle down to an urgent task, try lying down on the floor and covering yourself with a blue sheet or blanket. Breathe in the color blue, firstly to your throat chakra and then throughout your head. Continue until you feel your mind has come to rest and you have your powers of concentration back.

Breathe in blue energy

Feel blue's calming influence all over

Feel the red warmth spreading

151

Absent Healing

Candle
Lighting a candle in the same color can aid the sending of healing.

Absent healing is exactly what it says—it is healing someone in their absence, by means of meditation or visualization. In the case of color, it involves mentally transmitting color to the other person.

It is a good idea for the two people involved to link up, by agreeing on a mutually convenient time for the healing to take place. Then the person who is being healed by this method can be open to receiving it. You can also link in other ways. It is a good idea for both people to light a candle of the color being used in the healing.

Having faith

You can send healing to someone even if you do not link up, although it is probably more effective if you do. You should be careful, though, of sending healing to someone who does not want it or does not believe in it. They may not welcome it, or may think it intrusive, even if they are ill or unhappy. Absent healing works best when someone asks for it or agrees to it. It helps, too, if they are open to the process; a skeptical attitude can block the healing.

Creating what we think

If you believe that absent healing will work, there is a very good chance that it will. We tend to create what we think in our lives, which is why positive thinking is so important. If we go around with negative expectations of what will happen to us, our worst fears are likely to be fulfilled. If, on the other hand, we believe that things will turn out for the best, then we are likely to attract more positive experiences. As the saying goes, "it's all in the mind."

Sometimes the recipient of the absent healing may be too ill or depressed to actively cooperate with you. However, they may still feel the effect of the color and just knowing that someone else is thinking of them and doing something to help them, even if it is from a distance, can be a form of healing in itself.

Radionics

This complementary therapy is also a form of absent healing. Developed in the United States in the 1920s by Albert Abrams, radionics relies on using an instrument called a "black box" to analyze the vibratory patterns of a "witness" (an item belonging to the patient, such as a lock of hair or drop of blood), to diagnose health problems.

These are then treated by transmitting healing radiations through the witness. The treatment given follows holistic principles, treating all aspects of the patient's physical, mental, and emotional state. Radionics is a controversial therapy, though adherents claim to have treated many ailments successfully.

SENDING COLOR HEALING

If you wish to send a healing color to someone else, then prepare yourself in the same way as for meditation or visualization, taking deep breaths to relax the body and still the mind. Then picture the person you want to send healing to in your mind's eye; you may well find yourself "tuning in" to them or "feeling" their presence. Use a photograph of them if it helps you to concentrate.

Sending healing

1 Visualize the person to whom you are sending the healing or use a photograph of them if it helps you focus.

2 Open your chakras—ideally the other person should do the same—and bring in the color needed. You might be focusing on a specific condition or emotional state, or be doing this just for overall well-being. Refer to pages 22–93 if you are in any doubt about which color to use. You can also dowse for the color needed, or simply send white light, which of course contains all the colors of the spectrum.

3 Imagine the color radiating out from you to the other person. Beam it onto them like a laser, so that they are bathed in color; or direct it to a particular part of their body where you know they are experiencing pain or discomfort. Golden yellow is a good color to send—they will take from it what they need. Don't forget to close down your chakras when you have finished.

Send out a beam of color

154

Receiving healing

If you have linked up with each other, then the other person can also imagine the color being sent to them and this will aid the healing process. The whole session need not take very long; with practice, you will know when to stop and may even feel when the other person has had as much as they need. If they are going through a particularly bad time in their life, or are suffering from some kind of ongoing illness, you can make a regular appointment with them and send healing color each time.

6pm Tuesday
Tina's blood pressure up
again. Seeing doctor
tomorrow. Send healing.

Regular healing

The other person may want you to send healing to them on a regular basis.

Imagines
color
being sent

Relaxed and
receptive

The Laying On of Hands

Healing process
Touching someone with your hands is a very effective part of the color healing process.

In this form of healing the hands of one person are used to channel color to another person. We all unconsciously use our hands for healing ourselves and others. Instinctively we put out a hand to soothe and comfort someone in pain or distress. If we ourselves have a headache or a stomach pain, we immediately put a hand on the spot without even thinking about it, while if someone we know is upset then we often react by laying a hand on them or putting an arm around them. Human touch has great healing power.

Preparation

If you are the one who will be doing the healing, then it is important for you to prepare yourself as you would for meditation or visualization. You should also make sure that your hands are warm before laying them on someone else. The recipient should sit or lie down in a position in which they feel comfortable and close their eyes, to help them relax. Then place your right hand over their solar plexus and your left over the chakra that corresponds to the part of their body where the pain or the problem is. Visualize the color that is needed and imagine it flowing down your arm and into your right hand. It will then circulate through the other person's nervous system, and will finally complete the circuit at your left hand.

Colors to use

You may wish to use one of the blue colors because the other person is feeling stressed and is not sleeping well or is suffering from tension headaches. If, however, their physical vitality is low and they are lacking in confidence, then use red/orange. Use yellow if they are depressed or green if they have difficulty in relating to other people. Again, if you are not sure what color to use, refer to the section on Colors of the Spectrum (see pages 22–93).

When you become adept at this kind of color healing, you will know when the circuit has been completed and the right moment at which you should withdraw your left hand. Once you have taken it off, you should then shake it vigorously, to get rid of any negative vibrations that you may have picked up. It is also important to wash your hands after every treatment to make sure that no residue is left.

Conviction

It is important that the recipient of healing is open to the power of the laying on of hands, and the ability of the healer to channel healing color energies. Without this openness to the process on the part of the recipient, the chances of a successful outcome are reduced.

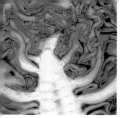

Food color

The color of food is one of the reasons we are drawn to it.

COLOR YOU EAT

Color is one of the attributes of food, along with aroma, texture, and taste, that stimulates our appetite and gets us salivating. What's more, we often instinctively choose to eat food for the properties associated with its color; for example, we eat oranges as a tonic when we have a cold, and red meat if we need an energy boost when we are feeling tired or have physical work to do.

Nutrients

The color of food also describes the nutrients that it contains; the vitamins and minerals that we need for healthy living. Once we know what these are, we can tailor our diet to what our bodies need on a day-to-day basis. It is a known fact that what we eat is a major contributing factor to good or ill health; and that some foods should be avoided if we are suffering from certain conditions, while others can be sought out for their healing properties.

A balanced diet

There are many different kinds of diets, some of them aimed at those who want to lose weight, others designed to alleviate specific conditions like cancer or arthritis. But if you adhere to a diet that includes food from each of the main groups—carbohydrates, fruit and vegetables, meat, fish, and other proteins, and some fats—in varying proportions, you will be ingesting all the colors of the spectrum.

Seasonal variations

There will be times when you need to eat more of one kind of food than another, depending on the season, the weather, and your own health, stress level, or mood. The following pages are designed to help you pinpoint, using color, the foods that you need for particular conditions or states of mind.

What Color Do You Eat?

Looking at food
*Look at the color of the food
that you eat—is it the color
that you need?*

The questionnaire on this page is designed to make you think carefully about the colors of the food that you eat, so take a few moments with a pen and paper to answer it. If you discover there is a color missing from your fruit bowl or vegetable rack, you will need to consider the properties it possesses (refer to Colors of the Spectrum on pages 22–93 if you need to refresh your memory). The absence of a color and lack of a nutrient may be causing physical, mental, or emotional problems.

Missing colors

If the questionnaire reveals that a certain color tends not to feature in the food that you normally eat, does the missing color relate to a particular complaint that you have? Do you, for example, tire easily or suffer from anemia? It may be that there is not enough red food in your diet.

Red food contains iron and you may need to increase your consumption of liver and kidney, for example. If these foods are distasteful to you, you can substitute them with spinach or watercress, which also contain iron. You may find that you sometimes get a sudden craving for these foods—this is a sure sign that your body is out of balance and needs the nutrients that they contain.

The color you eat the most

Think about the properties of the color that you eat the most—work out which specific property you feel you need and why. Do the same thing for all the food you normally eat, and that way, from the color alone, you will get a very good idea of whether your diet is balanced or not. If you feel it isn't, then you may need to include more green food in your diet—this will help you to counter any lack or excess.

While color can be a helpful guide to establishing which foods you need to eat more of, if you are in any doubt about your nutritional requirements, it is best to consult your doctor or a qualified dietician.

Questionnaire

What is the color of your favorite food?

What food don't you like and what color is it?

When you look in your vegetable rack, what colors do you see?

When you look in your fruit bowl, what colors do you see?

What colors are missing from both?

If you sometimes eat food on impulse, is it often of a specific color?

If you suffer from a particular condition, do you eat special food for it? If so, what color is it?

Feeling good
While your diet should contain a proportion of red, orange, and yellow food, too much can lead to an excess of energy.

RED, ORANGE, YELLOW FOOD

Red, orange, and yellow foods stimulate and energize our systems, cleanse and purify the blood, and boost our immune levels. They also earth us, helping us to root in the physical world and engage positively with life. We need them to recharge our batteries and to keep infection and disease at bay.

RED MEAT

Iron intake
If you are a vegetarian, eat plenty of green leafy vegetables to replace the red meat you have given up. These foods are categorized as "red" because they are also rich in iron.

SPINACH

Red food
Red food has already been mentioned as being important because it contains iron (see pages 160–161), essential for the formation of red blood cells and for keeping energy levels up. Even a mild deficiency of this mineral can lead to reduced work capacity and low resistance to disease.

Orange food

Orange food is associated with health and vitality, and in particular the all-important vitamin C, which is essential for overall good health. This vitamin can be found in citrus fruit. Carrots, another common orange food, contain beta-carotene, a major antioxidant that helps protect our defense system against air pollution. Honey, which is also an orange food, is good for the immune system.

PEACH

HONEY

CARROT

BANANA

Yellow food

Yellow food is important for the efficient functioning of the digestive system and for detoxifying the body in general. It's also good for the nervous system and the mental faculties, including reasoning, memory, and the ability to concentrate. Bananas, for example, one of the commonest yellow foods, are rich in potassium, and a deficiency in this mineral can lead to mental confusion and tiredness.

YELLOW LENTILS

LEMON

Cooking with Color

Warming

*Red, orange, and yellow food
helps to warm and invigorate us as
well as make us feel good.*

If you are lacking red, orange, or
yellow energy, it's quite easy to
introduce it into your diet. The foods
listed below will give you some ideas.

Red foods

• Tomatoes, red peppers, red
cabbage, beets, red chilies, kidney
beans, watercress, leafy dark green
vegetables (these contain iron which
qualifies them for this section).
• Black and white pepper, ginger,
cayenne pepper, rosemary, red sage.
• Red meat (do not eat to excess).

• Cherries, plums, rhubarb, apples,
raspberries, strawberries, redcurrants.

Orange foods
• Pumpkin, squash, turnip, carrots,
orange peppers.
• Coriander seeds, cumin.
• Orange lentils, egg yolks.
• Oranges, tangerines, peaches,
apricots, nectarines, mangoes,
pawpaws, melons.

Yellow foods
• Corn, squash, yellow peppers.
• Saffron, cinnamon, lemon grass, dill,
caraway.
• Yellow lentils, butter, oils, nuts, seeds,
whole grains.
• Pineapples, lemons, bananas,
grapefruit.

Recipe
Fall stew has been chosen for its red,
orange, and yellow ingredients.
It is a very warming, comforting, and
energizing dish to eat as the colder
days approach.

Fall Stew

Serves two to three

INGREDIENTS

Half a red pepper, chopped

1 can chopped tomatoes

1 red chili, deseeded and cut into
small pieces

1¼ cups (250g) split red lentils

half a medium-sized turnip, peeled
and cut into small pieces

3 medium-sized carrots,
peeled and sliced

2 potatoes, peeled and cubed

1 medium-sized onion, sliced

3 cloves garlic (or to taste)

2½ cups (550ml) water

¾ teaspoon (3.75 ml) turmeric

1 teaspoon (5ml) cumin seeds

1 teaspoon (5ml) coriander seeds

1 dozen juniper berries

1 banana, sliced, as garnish

2 tablespoons (15ml)
sunflower/olive oil

METHOD

Cover the lentils with cold water in a
large Dutch oven, then bring to a boil
and cook for 10 minutes, skimming the
surface as necessary. Put the lid on and
simmer for 15–20 minutes until the lentils
are a thick mush and all the liquid is
absorbed. While the lentils are cooking,
prepare the pepper, chili, turnip, carrots,
potatoes, onion, and garlic. Then fry the
vegetables in a separate pan in oil for
3–4 minutes, turning them all the time.

When the lentils are ready, ladle in the
vegetables together with the chopped
tomatoes and add the cumin and
coriander seeds as well as the juniper
berries. Simmer the mixture gently for
about an hour with the lid on until the
vegetables are cooked, but not too soft.

Serve the dish garnished with a sliced
banana. Fall stew is usually enough on its
own, but may be eaten with boiled rice,
flavored with ¾ tsp (3.75ml) of turmeric,
as desired.

Tomatoes contain a significant amount of
vitamin E, which guards against cancer
and heart disease; red pepper is high in
vitamins C and E, and beta-carotene.

Healthy

It's difficult to imagine that you could eat too much green food since it's essentially so healthy. But it does need to be combined with food of other colors for an optimum healthy diet.

GREEN FOOD

Green is the color of nature and so we view green food, such as salads, vegetables, fruit, and herbs as natural and healthy. These contain many of the vitamins and minerals that are necessary to keep our bodies in balance, which is another property of green. It's now widely accepted that a healthy diet should include at least five portions of fresh fruit and vegetables a day.

ICEBERG LETTUCE

BOSTON BIBB LETTUCE

Hearty food

Green is also the color that relates to the heart, and many green foods actually help to prevent heart disease. One of the causes of the disease is a diet low in the antioxidants vitamins C and E and beta-carotene. Green leafy vegetables are a particularly rich source of these. Lettuce is a good choice. It's best to buy organically grown if possible, since a lettuce's large expanse of leaf makes it particularly vulnerable to the chemicals that are used in fertilizers and pesticides. Therefore, if you do buy nonorganic varieties always rinse them well before eating. Do not throw away the outer leaves, since these contain higher levels of vitamins than the inner leaves. The packets of lettuce leaves that are ready-washed and torn, although convenient, have already lost much of their goodness.

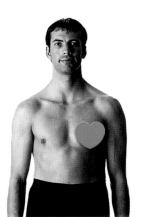

CURLY LEAF LETTUCE

BABY ROMAINE LETTUCE

Cooking with Green

Vitamins and minerals
Green food is full of the vitamins and minerals we need for a healthy diet.

Green foods are good for the heart; they also lower blood pressure, relieve stress and tension, alleviate headaches, and help with emotional problems. Green is nature's balancing force, so foods of this color are particularly good for bringing the body into harmony.

Green foods

• Cabbage, lettuce, green peppers, zucchini, peas, celery, artichokes, string beans, broccoli, cucumber, avocado, watercress, asparagus.
• Parsley, tarragon, alfalfa, mint, cilantro, basil, chives.
• Green lentils, neutral foods including natural yogurt and tofu.
• Apples, pears, kiwi fruit, limes, grapes, gooseberries, greengages.

Recipe

Watercress is a deep rich green and it is one of the healthiest foods we can eat. It contains particularly high levels of antioxidants—vitamins C, E, and carotenes—as well as iron and potassium. This delicate, fragile little plant helps to reduce the risk of cancer, prevent infection, and counter anemia. It has a pungent peppery flavor and does not keep well, so is best used fresh. Try and obtain it from a watercress farm, since wild watercress is known to harbor parasites.

Other green ingredients in this recipe include aromatic chives and fennel, which has feathery fronds and a clean, fresh smell of aniseed. Fennel is particularly good for relieving colic and gas.

Watercress Soup

Serves two to three

INGREDIENTS

2 large bunches of fresh watercress, destalked

1–1½lbs (450–675g) potatoes, peeled and chopped

2 tablespoons of butter or 2 tablespoons (15ml) extra virgin olive oil

3¾ cups (850ml) vegetable stock

⅔ cup (150ml) sour cream

4 large scallions, finely chopped

handful of chives and a few chopped fennel leaves

squeeze of lemon

salt and freshly ground pepper to taste

METHOD

Destalk and chop the fresh watercress; peel and chop the potatoes and scallions. Melt the butter or heat the olive oil in a heavy deep pan with a handle, then add the scallions, potatoes, and watercress, stirring until they are well coated with the butter or oil. Add salt, cover, and let the vegetables sweat over a low heat for about 15–20 minutes, stirring periodically.

Add the stock, increase the heat, and simmer, covered, for about 10–15 minutes until the vegetables are tender. Remove from the heat, allow to cool, and then liquidize for a short period only, to keep the texture slightly rough and not too glossy. Return to the pan, stir in the sour cream, add a squeeze of lemon, and check the seasoning—very little pepper is needed.

Serve the soup either hot or cold, garnished with chives and fennel leaves.

Inspiration

*Blue, indigo, and violet
food is particularly
good to eat if you are
lacking in inspiration.*

BLUE, INDIGO, AND VIOLET FOOD

There is not such an abundance of blue, indigo, and violet food as there is of
other colored food, but it still forms an important part of a healthy diet. It is the
counter to red, orange, and yellow food and it therefore cools and calms; it is
also nourishing for the nervous system, brain, and the higher mental faculties.

EGGPLANT

Brain food

This kind of food includes blue- and
blackberries, purple-topped vegetables
such as some varieties of broccoli, and
red cabbage and onions. With the color
violet, we are coming around the color
wheel toward red again, so purple food
is also energizing, particularly mentally.

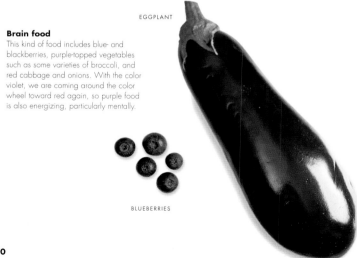

BLUEBERRIES

Sun ripened

Black or purplish-black grapes are one of the fruits that are included in this group of food. They are ripened on the vine, so when we eat them we are directly absorbing the rays of the sun. This also applies to other fruit and vegetables that are grown above ground. These should be eaten with their skins on, because this is the part that is exposed to the sun.

PURPLE-SKINNED ONION

BLACK GRAPES

Blue fish

Blue, indigo, and violet food also includes some fish, for example oily fish like mackerel and sardines, which have a bluish tinge to their scales. The benefits of this kind of fish have been well established by extensive research. Oily fish contains omega-3 fatty acids, which help to prevent heart disease and relieve rheumatoid arthritis. They are also high in vitamin D, which the body needs in order to absorb calcium, which is vital for bone growth.

MACKEREL

Cooking with Blue

Healthy desserts
*Even desserts can be healthy
if they contain ingredients with
vitamins that we need.*

I t is particularly good to introduce
blue, indigo, and violet food into your
diet if you have been through a very
stressful time and need to slow down;
or if you want to withdraw from the
busy outer world for a while.

Blue foods are cooling and soothing,
sedative, antiseptic, antifungal, and
bactericidal. Indigo foods too are
sedative; they also help with digestion,
purify, and stabilize. Violet foods are
good for nervous disorders, rheumatism,
and bladder troubles.

Blue, indigo, and violet foods
• Purple-leaved lettuce, eggplants,
sea vegetables, purple broccoli,
mushrooms, black olives.
• Blue sage, juniper berries.
• Black beans, black soybeans.
• Black grapes, blueberries, plums,
bilberries, blackberries, prunes, black
cherries, raisins, and currants.

Recipe
The berries that constitute the main
ingredient of this scrumptious Blue
Summer Pudding are rich in vitamins
and high in antioxidants. Blackberries
are an excellent source of vitamin E,
while blueberries are good for the
eyesight and, like blackcurrants, help
to prevent infections of the urinary tract.
Blackcurrants also contain a high level
of vitamin C.

To make the dish even more fun,
you can make the cream blue by
adding blue coloring to it, or, more
exotically, blue curaçao. Add blue
food coloring very sparingly. Finally,
decorate the pudding with blue flowers.

Blue Summer Pudding

Serves two to three

INGREDIENTS

1 cup (250g) blueberries

½ cup (125g) blackberries

½ cup (125g) blackcurrants

½ cup (100g) granulated sugar

several medium slices of one-day-old white bread

¼ cup (275ml) heavy cream

several drops of blue coloring, or 1–2 tablespoons (8–15ml) blue curaçao

2½–3¾ cups (600–850ml) pudding bowl or soufflé dish

edible blue flowers

METHOD

Rinse the fruit and place it in a large pan with the sugar and 1–2 tablespoons (8–15ml) of water to stop it from sticking to the bottom of the pan before the juice has been released. Cook gently for 4–5 minutes until the sugar melts and the juice runs—do not leave it for any longer or the fruit will get too mushy. Save the juice and put it to one side.

Cut the crusts off of the bread and line the bottom and the sides of the pudding bowl with the slices, slightly overlapping them and pressing them together to seal the dish completely. Add the fruit, then make a lid with more bread, again sealing the edges carefully all around. Place a saucer or small plate over the top to fit inside the rim of the bowl, so the fruit can be pressed down. Add 3lb (1.4kg) or 4lb (1.8kg) weights on top of the plate and refrigerate the dish overnight.

Turn the pudding out and brush the bread with the saved fruit juice to cover any remaining white patches. Decorate the top with candied violets, edible blue flowers such as lavender, borage, cornflowers, or pansies. Finally, add the blue coloring or blue curaçao to the cream and serve.

THE COLOR OF YOUR ENVIRONMENT

Color is personal; the clothes we wear and the color schemes of our homes and gardens all say a great deal about us. They indicate the state of our health, our mind, and describe our personalities. It is important to surround ourselves with colors to which we are attracted, so that we feel in tune with, and supported by, our environment. 🐦 It's also important to recognize that our need for color changes as we ourselves change; while we may always have a favorite color, there will be times when we have a sudden urge to redecorate a room or buy an article of clothing in a color that normally we would avoid. 🐦 This section of the book is designed to increase your awareness of what color you are most drawn to at any given time and to help you change the color of your environment to reflect that.

Color of Traditional Dress

Uniformity

Most school uniforms are in the colors of conformity: blue, gray, brown, and black.

Throughout history the properties of color have been used in the form of dress in order to reinforce people in their traditional roles in society. Royalty, high-ranking members of the clergy, and the judiciary, for example, have habitually donned purple, the color of nobility, dignity, and the highest form of self-expression. The color of uniforms of all kinds indicates the qualities needed in their work by the people who wear them.

Red, the color of courage, action, and aggression, has always been favored by the military, particularly for show. It is also the color of the blood that the fighting man spills. Blue, the color of the sea, is the color of naval uniforms, to the extent that navy blue is a color in itself. Gray, or blue-gray, is the color of the Royal Air Force uniform and is also the color of the aircraft its pilots fly as well as the skies they fly through. We can tell, just by looking at the color of the uniforms that these people wear, which roles they have and the qualities they need in order to perform them well.

Black, the color of authority and power, is worn by the police in Britain, who have to enforce the law against the criminal element of society; it is also the color of the habits worn by some religious orders, and here black carries the meaning of shutting out the external world, so that the wearer may focus on more spiritual concerns.

Business

The blue or gray of the suits worn by many businesspeople—another kind of uniform—convey the impression that these are sober, reliable people whom we can trust with our money or details of our affairs. The color of the uniforms worn by the staff of many companies is carefully chosen for the qualities associated with it—orange for zest and vitality, red and yellow for energy and stimulation, green for health, and so on.

School uniform

Even the colors of the uniforms that some schoolchildren wear—blue, gray, brown, black, and so on—are chosen to encourage conformity, rather than to reflect the energies of the individual. Given the constraints imposed upon many of us by the color we have to wear to work, it is small wonder that the first thing we do when we get home is to change into a color in which we feel we can be more ourselves.

Personal touch
Even if you wear a uniform at work, or clothes that conform to other people's expectations, you can still complement what you wear with an accessory—a tie, ring, scarf, or belt—in a color that you particularly like.

WHAT COLOR DO YOU WEAR?

The fabric of the clothes that we wear acts as a filter for color to be absorbed through the skin. For example, if you are wearing a green shirt, then you take in the properties of the color green. This gives rise to a sense of harmony with your surroundings and opens you up, and so on. It is therefore important that the colors you choose to wear reflect or enhance your natural energies, which of course vary from day to day.

What you don't wear
Think about the color you never wear, that's not represented in your wardrobe, and its particular properties. Refer to Colors of the Spectrum on pages 22–93 if you want to refresh your memory about the colors and what they stand for. If, for example, you never wear red, is it because you are naturally a "red" person and don't need that energy, or is it because you're lacking in energy, confidence, or initiative? If it is the latter, then wearing red can help you to develop these qualities.

Questionnaire

What color do you always wear?

How do you feel in it?

How do others react to you in it?

What color do you never wear? Why?

What color are you wearing now? Why did you choose it?

When you look at all your clothes, what colors dominate?

What colors are missing from your clothing collection?

Look at the clothes that you don't wear any more, what color are they?

What color would you like to wear but don't? Why not?

Have you recently bought something in a new color? What prompted you to do this?

Dark, bright, or neutral?

We tend to wear dark colors when we feel physically or emotionally low, bright colors when we are in high spirits, and neutral colors when we are tired and want to take it easy. The questionnaire on the left is designed to make you think about the colors that you wear or don't wear, so take a few moments to answer it using paper and pen.

Dark colors

Bright colors

Neutral colors

Your Natural Coloring

Skin color
*What goes with the color
of your skin influences the colors
that you choose to wear.*

Most of us, whether consciously or unconsciously, choose colors to wear that go with our natural coloring, i.e., the color of our skin, eyes, and hair. If we wear colors that clash with these, then we tend not to look our best and other people are quite likely to say that those particular colors do not suit us.

A German color theorist, Johannes Itten, categorized people of different coloring according to the four seasons of the year—spring, summer, fall, and winter. While not everyone falls neatly into these categories because we may be of mixed race or given to experimenting with the color of our hair—or even our eyes, in the form of colored contact lenses—they serve as a useful guide to the colors in which each of us looks and feels good. Read on to discover which season you fit into, and the colors that suit you best.

"Spring" and "summer" people

"Spring" people tend to have pink/ivory skin—the "peaches-and-cream" complexion is typical of this—blue or green eyes and golden blond or brown hair. They look good in light, pale colors such as pink, peach, lemon, cream, and green. These people are often lively, outgoing, and enthusiastic.

"Summer" people are also fair-skinned and often have pink complexions, commonly with pale blue or gray, but sometimes hazel, eyes and light blond or brown hair. The colors that look best on them are blue and pink. Summer people are dependable, cooperative, sensitive, and serious.

"Fall" and "winter" people

The coloring of "fall" people tends to be that of their season—red, brown, and gold. Their skin tone usually ranges from golden through tan to copper, and they also often have freckles. Their eyes are usually green or brown and their hair shades of red or brown. People of this type look best in rich fall colors—orange, yellow, and russet.

Many "winter" people are olive- or dark-skinned and have eyes of varying shades of brown. Their hair is usually dark brown or black. People of this type look good in strong, bright colors such as red, green, or purple, but they are also particularly suited to wearing black or white.

Chinese Seasons

In traditional Chinese medicine, each season has an associated color and element, which is linked to parts of the body. Each seasonal type of person therefore has a tendency to weakness in certain health areas. For winter people, these include the urinary system; for spring people, the liver; for summer people, the heart; for fall people, the lungs.

COLORS FOR LEISURE WEAR

While the clothes we wear to the office may have to conform to the colors of the company or the institution that employs us, away from the workplace we can wear the colors that we particularly like. There are colors, however, that are especially good for certain activities. Whatever you decide to do with your leisure time, the colors that you wear can not only help to reflect your mood, but can also help to create it.

Chill out

If you have spent the day in dark business clothes, you might feel like changing into one of the lighter, softer colors when you get home. Blue will soothe you and help you unwind, while pink will give you a good feeling about yourself. Gray induces a feeling of space, and is good if you just need to hang out.

Blue aids relaxation

Loose, comfortable clothes

Light color

The colors at the warm end of the spectrum are also good to wear if you are socializing after work and want to liven yourself up.

Red or orange

*Red will give you the
confidence to go up to
people that you do not
know, and orange will put
you in a party mood.*

Yellow

*Yellow will get you
talking to others.*

Energy boost

If you are one of those people who likes to go to the gym or for a run after work, you might opt to change into an energetic color like red or orange, particularly if you have had a tiring day. They will give you the boost that you need for strenuous physical exercise.

Mental stimulation

If you intend to spend the evening studying, perhaps for a course or an exam that you are taking, you might want to put on something yellow, to stimulate your mind.

Natural Versus Synthetic Fibers

Synthetic material
Many modern clothes are made of synthetic material, but the skin cannot breathe through them.

I t is not only the color that we wear that is important to our well-being, but also the quality of the fabric itself. Whether a fabric is natural or synthetic will make a very big difference to how we feel when wearing it.

Synthetic, or manmade, fibers have been popular since World War II, because they make possible the manufacture of mass-market clothing at prices everyone can afford. Nylon, the first and best known of the synthetic fibers, has become synonymous with one of the products for which it is used, ladies' panty hose. However, synthetic fibers are produced by chemically processing raw materials like wood pulp and petroleum extracts and these do not allow the skin to breathe. Also, light cannot penetrate the fabric in the same way as through natural fibers.

Silk

Perhaps the most sensuous of natural fibers is silk, and after thousands of years of people wearing it, it is still considered a luxury material. Silk is the stuff of cocoons that are made by certain species of caterpillars and for many centuries its main producer, China, shrouded its production in secrecy. Apart from its sheen and softness to the touch, silk has another important quality: its fibers reflect light like a prism and it has high absorbency, enabling it to be dyed with a range of deep, brilliant colors. This makes silk one of the most effective fabric conductors of color energy.

Cotton

Cotton is one of the most common of all textile fibers and its history goes back thousands of years. A product of the cotton plant, it is a clean, fresh fabric that feels very comfortable next to the skin. Cotton is very versatile, because it can be woven in any texture and dyed in any color. It allows the skin to breathe, and light to reach the skin.

Wool

Wool is a fiber that is made from the fleece or hair of various animals and it can include alpaca, mohair, cashmere, and camel. The making of wool was a major industry in ancient Babylon and Mesopotamia. Wool contains tiny air pockets that insulate the body and it is also easy to dye. It too, lets in light and so allows the body to absorb color.

Presentation skills
If you have an important
presentation to make and
therefore want to express
yourself clearly in order to
get your message across,
try adding a touch of yellow
to what you are wearing.

COLORS FOR WORKWEAR

The color that you wear at work depends to some extent on the conventions of business dress—this has traditionally been narrower for men than for women, since women can generally get away with wearing much brighter colors. However, this is now changing and the most important points to consider are what your career is, and what impression you want to create.

Approachability
If your job involves a lot of
direct dealing with people,
perhaps in a helping or
counseling capacity, it is
best to wear softer, warmer
colors. Pink or peach, for
example, will help people to
feel comfortable with you.
Green, blue, and turquoise
are also good colors
to wear because they will
help you to empathize with
people and give you an
insight into their problems.

Red instils confidence

Orange shows a sense of humor

Black denotes power and authority

Leadership

If your role is that of a leader, you may choose to wear black, which bestows authority and power. However, this can also intimidate, so it is best if it is worn with an accessory in a color. Red will encourage your team to have confidence in your leadership and will get them pulling behind you, while orange will show that you are young at heart and that you have a good sense of humor.

Appropriate clothing

Whatever your job, and whatever is on the agenda for the day, take a moment to think about the appropriate color to wear when you dress in the morning—it could make all the difference to your day.

Colors That You Don't Wear

Underwear
The color of your underwear can also help you feel the way you want to.

The color that you don't wear could be the color to which you need to pay the most attention. It may well be that you have outgrown it now; it represents a stage in your life that you have moved on from and that's why you no longer wear clothes of that color. If you have a pile of clothes that you have not worn for a year, either because they do not fit well, are no longer fashionable, you do not like them, or you no longer like the color, then get of them. Take them to a goodwill outlet or give them to a friend so they don't clutter up your life any more.

Colors that fight back

Alternatively, it may be that you tend to express the negative side of the qualities that the particular color represents. It could be yellow: when this energy is working well in you, you think clearly, the ideas come, and you communicate well with others. But if it's not, you may find yourself continually picking fault with other people and taking a cynical view of things, which makes you unpopular. You may not have the skin tone for yellow—it goes best with sallow or darker-colored skin—but you can always wear a touch of yellow (for example, a scarf) as an accessory to help you develop the color's positive traits.

Color compromises

If you really dislike a color and cannot see yourself in it at all, you can always wear it as underwear. For example, maybe you feel red is just too much for you to wear, but at the same time you want to become more assertive at work. Try wearing some red underwear to help you stand up for yourself. It will also keep you warm!

You can also wear a shade or a tint of the color that you don't like—choose pink or magenta as a substitute for red; apricot or peach instead of orange; and lilac or lavender as a replacement for purple. A substitute shade or tint will not have as strong an effect as the unadulterated color, but it will still influence the way that you feel.

However, it's important that you don't wear a color that you don't like simply because it happens to be in fashion: follow your heart rather than the dictates of fashion (and that goes for choice of clothes, too).

Building blocks
Look around your personal environment with fresh eyes and think about the color you live with, so that it truly reflects the color you are.

COLOR THAT YOU LIVE WITH Our

own home is where we take sanctuary from the world; we return to it at the end of a day's work, and also eat, sleep, make love, relax with family and friends, and recuperate after illness there. In short, it is the place where we spend a large part of our lives and so it's important that the color we live with supports us physically, emotionally, mentally, and spiritually.

Color transformations
You may not have given much thought to the colors you are surrounded by; you may have lived with the same colors for years, never really taking them in or pausing to consider whether they truly reflect who you are. At the same time you may be aware of not liking a particular room, because it's too small, too dark, or too cold. Color can help to transform such an environment, turning a room you avoid, or use for storing junk, into a space that supports you in whatever activity you choose to do in there.

Paint samples

If you want some ideas, walk around your home with a swatch of paint samples.

Follow your instincts

You don't have to spend a fortune on expensive interior designers or decorating materials to get your home looking the way that you want it to. Paint can be obtained quite inexpensively and most of us can pick up a brush and slap some on a wall. The important thing is to choose the colors you want, not what is fashionable or what other people think you should have. Your favorite color, or a color you need to have around you to reflect who you are at a particular time in your life, may be a color that someone else can't stand.

What Colors Do You Live With?

Taking it in
Have a good look round the place where you live and take in all the colors.

Take a few moments with pen and paper to answer the questionnaire on the next page. You could also try wandering through the rooms in your flat or house, looking around you at the color you live with and thinking about the questions asked. Look up and down as well as around you— look at the ceiling above your head and the floor beneath your feet. You should also take in the furnishings, pictures, and books on the shelves

and check your instinctive reaction to the colors you see. Is there too much of one color? Not enough of another? Is the overall effect too dark, too light, too bright, or too dull?

It may be that as you look around you, a color comes into your mind— remember it; it may be a color that you need at this point in your life, to reflect a change in yourself or your circumstances. Perhaps, for example, you now work from home instead of going out to an office; or maybe someone has moved in, or out.

What the room is for

You also need to consider what each room is for and whether its color scheme serves that purpose. Take your bedroom, for example. How well do you sleep in it? Do you wake up refreshed in the morning after a good night's sleep or do you surface feeling tired after waking up in the middle of the night and tossing and turning? If the latter, it may be that your bedroom is in one of the colors at the warm end of the spectrum, which are very stimulating, while you need a cool, calm blue. You can ask yourself the same kind of question for each room as you go around your home. Is the living room a place where people relax and talk or is it somewhere they argue? How much work do you get done in your study? What color would help to change things? Refer to the section on Colors of the Spectrum (on pages 22–93) if you're not sure what particular color to use, but, above all, be guided by your own intuition.

Questionnaire

What is the main color of the room you are in?

How do you feel in this room?

How do other members of your family/friends behave in this room? Do they act aggressively? Are they restless or relaxed?

Is it in a color you like? If not, what color would you change it to?

Complementary colors
Colors can be used not only on their own, but also to complement each other.

LIVING ROOM AND BEDROOM

The living room is one of the focal areas in any home; it's the place where the occupants congregate, socialize, watch TV, read, and generally "hang out." So it's a room that has to perform several different functions, all of which need to be taken into account when planning its color scheme.

Creating an atmosphere

The main thing to consider when you begin to plan is what kind of atmosphere you wish to create—whether you wish it to be quiet and peaceful or warm and welcoming. If the latter, you will need to introduce colors from the warm end of the spectrum, perhaps peach or apricot—tints of orange, which is a joyful and expansive color. Either of these would go well with blue, the complementary color to orange, and this combination would create an environment in which people can relax in each other's company. The effect can be enhanced by cushions, throws, and pictures in varying tones of the two colors.

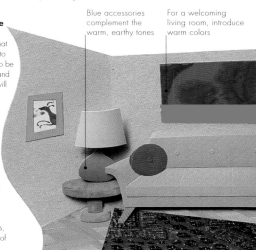

Blue accessories complement the warm, earthy tones

For a welcoming living room, introduce warm colors

A restful room

The bedroom is another very important room because that's where we sleep, make love, think, read, and perhaps write. It's essentially a private room, whether you retire there to be alone or to be intimate with another person. So it's a room which, perhaps more than any other, needs to be decorated in colors that reflect who you are.

Primarily the colors you use need to be restful so that you can get a good night's sleep. Pink is a popular color for bedrooms as it's soft and gentle and will make you feel supported. You can also use tints of white rather than white on its own which can look and feel a bit clinical (see pages 80–81). Blue is a tranquil color, but is not the best choice if your room is cold, because it will make it seem even colder.

SCENTED CANDLES

CANDLE

OIL BURNER

RED LINEN

Passionate touches

If you want to create a setting for passionate lovemaking, you can always introduce red into the decor, although this is best done in the form of sheets or candles and colored lightbulbs, otherwise you are unlikely to be able to get a good night's sleep.

Connecting Spaces

Impression
Even the color of your front door will give your visitors a particular impression.

There are many other spaces in a house besides rooms and these mainly consist of connecting spaces like entrance halls, staircases, landings, and passages. These spaces connect in more than one sense since they are spaces that people move through on their way from one part of the house to another, as well as using them to linger in for a quick chat, a gossip, or a hastily imparted confidence.

These spaces are places of activity and are also often the first part of your home that people will see. So, what impression do you want them to get? Dramatic, warm, and welcoming, or a haven from the world? Bright, vibrant colors from the warm end of the spectrum will welcome them into your home and make them feel a part of it. If you want to create a softer, cozier effect, you can always use tints or shades of these colors, such as terra-cotta or rust for red or orange, and lemon for yellow. It is also important to pay attention to the color that you paint the front door. In some cultures, it is always painted in a protective color, such as black, white, purple, or blue.

If, on the other hand, you work long hours in a demanding job, you may just want to shut the door on the world and collapse when you get home at night. If so, colors from the cool end of the spectrum will help you to unwind the moment you step inside.

Neutral colors

Communal areas are often painted in neutral colors such as off-white, cream, or beige, but these can make for a static atmosphere, where strangers visiting your home just huddle inside the front door, not knowing whether to advance or not.

Sometimes these connecting areas of our homes are small, cramped spaces without much natural light and they may also be stuffy and cold. Different colors can help to counter this: pastel colors, for example, will create a light, spacious effect, while dark or rich colors will make a space more intimate. A cold corridor can be made to seem warmer by the use of a color from the red end of the spectrum. An airless landing will seem cooler and fresher if a color from the blue end of the spectrum is used.

Feng Shui

According to the Chinese practice of Feng Shui, the position of your staircase affects the chi (energy) present in the house. It is not good if a staircase starts directly in front of the front door. Curving stairs are preferable to straight, spiral staircases are not recommended, and steps should be solid and always covered.

Bright colors
Bright colors in the kitchen will help create a warm, inviting atmosphere.

THE KITCHEN AND BATHROOM

The kitchen and bathroom are two contrasting rooms, in which very different kinds of activities take place. The kitchen is not only the place where food is cooked, it is often also where the family gathers together for a meal and where we entertain friends. The bathroom is a much more private room to which we may like to retreat for a long hot soak at the end of a tiring day.

Heart of the home
The kitchen is the hub of the house and so the colors used here need to reflect warmth and conviviality. Red will energize; orange will whet the appetite and aid the digestion; and yellow will stimulate conversation. Red also earths us and so a kitchen floor made up of terra-cotta tiles, for example, will help us to find our feet after a day spent in front of a computer or at meetings with other people. The kitchen also offers plenty of scope for splashes of contrasting or complementary color in the form of bowls of fruit and vegetables, plants, displays of crockery, and so on.

Inviting bathrooms

Many bathrooms are small, poky places without even a window. This makes it even more important to choose colors that will make the room look lighter and larger, such as blues and turquoise, the colors of the sea, which will help to relax and soothe you. The bathroom is not a place where you want to feel cold, however, so these need to be offset by softer, warmer colors in the form of a rug, bathmat, towels, or bathrobe.

Blue

Shades of blue in the bathroom will help put you in a relaxing frame of mind.

Blue and turquoise decor

Soft peach accessories

Warm-toned lamp

Other Rooms

Working at home
*The color of your study or studio
can make all the difference to
how your work goes.*

There are, of course, other rooms
in the house, such as a study or
conservatory. The study area may
be a corner of another room or a loft
specially converted for the purpose.
Studies are often used for hobbies, or
for children to do their homework. Until
recently, it was probably considered
something of a luxury to have a room
in the house devoted entirely to the
pursuit of some fascinating hobby.
Nowadays, however, as more and
more people work from home, it is
increasingly a necessity.

Working from home

It may be that you don't have a big
enough apartment or house to be able
to set aside a room solely for work, but
even if you use a space within another
room, you still need to think about what
color is going to inspire you and
maximize your productivity.

If, for example, your work is of a
mental rather than physical nature,
involving thinking, reading, writing,
and coming up with ideas, then yellow
is a wonderful color for stimulating the
mind. Being the color closest to the light
of the sun, it will also help to keep up
your spirits as you work.

If your work is of an artistic nature—
drawing, painting, or sewing, for
example—then you might want to
place purple around you. This is the
color of creative inspiration and it will
also help keep the distractions of the
outer world at bay.

If space allows, you might want to
set aside a corner to rest or meditate,
and for this cool blues, greens, and
turquoise would be best.

Children's rooms

Children very often need an area
of their room set aside for study,
particularly as they get older. As they
grow and develop, they tend to be
attracted to stronger and brighter
colors, which reflect their abundance
of energy. However, these bold, bright
colors are not conducive to quiet study,
so it is best to partition off a corner of
their room and decorate it in paler,
softer colors that will encourage them
to concentrate when homework has
to be done.

If your child experiences difficulty
in sleeping, make sure that this is not
because the room's color scheme is
too bright and overstimulating.

Pattern Power

Be careful when buying bedding for a child's
room. Its color vibrations will penetrate the
aura of a sleeping child.

Pay attention to what is printed on the
bedding, too. Large, vibrantly colored
designs or bold figures can emit negative
vibrational energies.

Harmonize with nature

You can create a garden, however small, with colors in it that will change throughout the year to reflect the seasons and your own shifting moods.

COLOR IN THE GARDEN

Gardens are very healing places, not only because they bring us into contact with nature, but also because of the colors of the plants, flowers, and shrubs. Even if you live in the city and can boast only a tiny border and a strip of concrete for a garden, you can still plant it up with colors that will heal and inspire you all year round.

Seasonal colors

Color does not easily divide into the four seasons of the year any more than many plants do. Yet it is possible to distinguish the pale, promising colors of spring from the brilliant, ripe colors of summer, and the dying shades of fall from the stark contrasts of winter.

Seasons

Changes in the garden will keep you in touch with the seasons.

Contrasting colors

Complementary colors can work just as well in the garden as in the home.

Warm colors

Warm colors like orange can be a joy to look at on a gray day.

Plants and Flowers for Spring

Welcome sight
After the barrenness of winter, the early flowers of spring are a welcome sight.

The flower that we probably associate most with spring is the common snowdrop, whose flowers show dramatically white against the dark ground and bare trees of late winter. But snowdrops can actually flower for up to five months, from fall and winter to early spring. However, after the long, dark days of winter, they are seen as a herald of the light to come and so we think of them as spring flowers. The shrub magnolia also symbolizes spring, whether it is the pink-flowering variety or M. *stellata*, the star magnolia, so-called because of its star-shaped white flowers. These can be grown in the smallest of gardens and look good planted next to camellias, particularly of the 'Donation' variety. The attractive green foliage and large soft pink flowers of camellias are one of the finest displays of spring.

Azaleas

Azaleas, a form of rhododendron, also flower in late spring and can be grown in large tubs. They come in two varieties, evergreen (also known as Japanese) and deciduous. The color of the former ranges through most of the colors of the rainbow—from white through pink, red, and vermilion to blue, lilac, and purple. The deciduous azaleas have a similar range of colors, with the addition of yellow and orange. The species *Rhododendron luteum* produces a golden flower with a particularly fragrant scent.

Spring bulbs

Spring would not be spring without daffodils, narcissi, crocuses, and tulips. If you have a large enough garden, create a wild, woodland effect by scattering the bulbs haphazardly under the trees. In spring you will be rewarded by an unforgettable sight.

Crocuses come in many different varieties, in colors ranging from white to golden yellow and purple. Early-flowering tulips come in a similar range of colors, including white and yellow, which are, more than any other, the colors of spring. Some varieties of cyclamen also flower in spring. They vary from white to pink and deep red.

Daffodils

Daffodils are adaptable plants that are happy in shady areas as well as in full sun. Plant the bulbs to a depth of twice the height of the bulb, spacing them 4–8in (10–20cm) apart, in early to mid-fall. They are best planted in groups or drifts. Let the leaves die back naturally after flowering.

*Summer is a time
when the garden
is ablaze with color
from many different
plants.*

THE GARDEN IN SUMMER Summer is a
long season, spanning late spring and early fall. This is reflected in the colors
of summer, which range from the pastels of spring to the rich warm colors of
fall. At the height of this season, color in the garden really comes into its own,
as there is an overwhelming variety of herbaceous plants of all kinds and
colors as well as a myriad of greens from trees in full leaf.

Blossoming forth
In late spring the first roses
can already be seen and
many shrubs are also
coming into season.
Geraniums, are starting to
bud and a host of annuals are
producing their first flowers.
In early summer, the day is at
its longest and lightest and the
garden is bursting with growth
of every kind. Midsummer brings
forth the climbers—rose, clematis,
and jasmine—in a tangle of
white, pink, and blue, while in
late summer the later-flowering
plants are beginning to take
over the garden. By early fall
it's time to plant ahead.

Herbaceous plants

Herbaceous plants,
perennials which flower
for several years at least,
come into their own during
the summer months.

JASMINE

ROSE

Sweet scents

Summer is a time when we
may sate our senses with the
brilliant colors and heady
scents of a profusion of
plants and flowers.

Plants and Flowers for Summer

Primula
The primula will grow in most gardens and helps to postpone the end of summer.

Reigning supreme over summer is the rose, which ranges in color from deep red to yellow and creamy white. The flowers may be single or what are known as full doubles, where the petals are packed together in layers to form a soft, cushiony, sensuous ball. Many varieties also have a divine scent, which is enough to send the senses reeling. Roses are generally at their best in early to midsummer, although some varieties have a second, less fulsome flowering later in the year.

A subtler fragrance is emitted by the small, delicate, pale mauve-pink flowers of the jasmine 'Stephanense', which is often to be found growing side by side with the common white jasmine, which flowers all summer long. Another popular climber is the clematis, which comes in a variety of colors from white, light and dark pink, to blue, mauve, and deep purple.

Primulas flower throughout the length of the summer in strong reds, deep purple, yellow, and orange. If you have water in your garden, they will do well growing at the edge, since they thrive in a combination of moisture and shade.

Herbaceous plants

Herbaceous plants (those that die back each winter and grow again in spring) provide an endless source of color throughout the summer months. They include lupins, whose tall spires flower in a range of colors—white, blue, pink, violet, red, and yellow—as well as day lilies and carnations. Pink and red sweet williams lend a homely air to the garden, while the vivid red, orange, and yellow of California and Iceland poppies light it up.

Hydrangeas

Hydrangeas take us from summer into fall and reflect the changing of the seasons in their flowers and colors. The flowers' texture goes from silky to waxy and their colors turn from blue to a light pale green, red to brown, and from white to greenish-white. There are two kinds of hydrangeas, mopheads—so-called because of their large floppy heads of flowers—and lacecaps, whose flowers are flatter. The mopheads suitable for a small garden are the sky-blue 'Vibraye' and the dwarf 'Pia', whose red flowers take us well into fall.

Keats
The poet wrote of fall as "the season of mists and mellow fruitfulness."

THE GARDEN IN FALL
When there begins to be a chill in the air and the leaves of the trees start to turn, we know that fall is on its way. The poignancy of this time of year is heightened by the flare of color in the foliage of the trees, which is a final show put on by nature before the light sinks to its lowest and winter sets in.

Fall colors
To take a walk through woods in fall is to be treated to a blaze of red, orange, yellow, gold, copper, and russet, accentuated by the green of conifer, fern, and moss. A shaft of sunlight striking through the trees and illumining the veins of leaves is a sight to fill us with awe.

Transition

*Fall is a time of transition, from ripe summer to
bare winter, when we pause to reflect on what
has passed and what is to come.*

Plants and Flowers for Fall

Heather
Heathers flower throughout fall in colors to match the foliage of the trees.

Some shrubs flower well into fall and among them is the hardy fuchsia, which bears clusters of dangling flowers in a voluptuous magenta. These flowers contrast particularly well with the tall, creamy spikes of the exotic yucca. The hardy hibiscus produces flowers in purplish-red, bluish-purple, and white, while an unseasonal and spectacular splash of bright yellow is provided by the evergreen *Hypericum* 'Hidcote'.

Heather is a feature of fall, and this looks its best when planted massed together, so that the traditional greens and grays we associate with this shrub set off the pink flowers and orange foliage of varieties like 'Orange Queen' or the white flowers and yellow foliage of 'Gold Haze'.

Japanese maples

One of the stars of fall is undoubtedly the Japanese maple, as its turning leaves provide an unmatched display of rich gold, bright scarlet, and canary yellow. The North American tupelo tree adds orange to this show, while among the mountain ashes the *Sorbus* 'Embley' is renowned for its striking red leaves. The tiny *Sorbus reducta*, which seldom grows to a height of more than 1 foot (30cm), will provide even the smallest of gardens with red and purple fall color, as well as white fruits. This is, after all, the season of hips and berries and among the best of the fruiting roses is the *rugosa*, which produces bright red hips the size of small tomatoes.

Fall bulbs

Fall-flowering bulbs are not as well known as spring bulbs, with the exception of cyclamen, which flowers pink and white in early fall. One of the most beautiful bulbs is the nerine, in particular *Nerine bowdenii*, which is hardy and easy to grow. It produces clusters of the most delicate fairy-pink flowers that turn outward at the tips in a feminine curve.

Among fall-flowering herbaceous plants are Japanese anemones, which range in color from white and cream to pink and rose. Michaelmas daisies are popular, the most noticeable is *Aster* 'Frikartii', which is distinguished by flowers of a lavender-blue. Finally chrysanthemums create a mass of color in apricot and bronze, and white, yellow, pink, and red.

Berries and cones
There may be fewer flowers in winter, but there are berries and cones galore.

THE GARDEN IN WINTER

In winter everything seems to come to a standstill. The ground turns hard and may be covered with the white rime of frost or snow, the herbaceous plants have long died, and the deciduous trees and shrubs shed their leaves. Animals hibernate and the days grow shorter and darker.

Winter color
At this time of year there is little color from flowers in the garden, but a variety of greens is provided by the conifers and splashes of bright red and yellow by the berries of various shrubs. The black skeletal outlines of trees also contrast sharply with the leaden skies of winter and fallen snow.

Frost
Winter has its own special beauty, as in these leaves outlined by frost.

Winter landscape
The whiteness of the snow and the darkness of the Earth throw everything in the winter landscape into sharp definition.

Conserving energy
Winter is a time for turning inward, whether seated before the leaping flames of a log fire, or on a brisk walk through a mute, starkly beautiful landscape. It is a time for conserving our strength, like the animal and plant life around us, until the light returns in the spring.

Holly
Holly brings a touch of festive green to our homes.

COLOR HEALING

SECRETS

215

Plants and Flowers for Winter

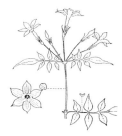

Standing out
Color in winter stands out all the more for being scarcer than at other times.

The cold, crisp air of winter is scented by the large white or cream flowers of the hybrid honeysuckle as well as by daphnes, whose purplish-pink flowers are followed by black fruits, and the viburnum 'Dawn', whose red buds open to white flowers flushed with pink. Lighting the darkness of winter with its large yellow flowers is the winter jasmine, which looks its best when trailed over a trellis or wall. The evergreen clematis also flowers all winter long, producing blooms of a whitish-yellow. Winter color is also provided by crocuses in white, pale and dark yellow, blue, mauve, and purple as well as by winter-flowering pansies, which range from white to a rich, dark red.

Mahonias are particularly noticeable for their striking evergreen foliage. One of the most beautiful is *Mahonia japonica*, whose stiff, spiny leaves are complemented by clusters of pendulous yellow flowers. This mahonia will flower throughout winter and also bears berries of purple or black.

Holly and ivy

If there is a dearth of color from flowers in winter, it is in part made up for by the berries that are produced by various shrubs. Pyracanthas, which will grow in almost any soil, produce a wealth of red, orange, and yellow fruits throughout the winter. Other berrying shrubs include cotoneaster and of course holly, which is synonymous with the great festival of winter, Christmas. There are many species of holly with a variety of leaves, ranging from the large, shiny, and spineless evergreen to the variegated gold kind. We tend to think of the berries as red, but they can also be yellow.

Ivies come into their own during the winter and their leaves trail everywhere in a range of variegated colors— green, yellow, silver, gray, and white. They go well with holly, as celebrated in the carol "The Holly and the Ivy," and a traditional Christmas would seem incomplete without these two stalwarts of winter.

Hellebores

An ideal variety of hellebore for a winter planting is *Helleborus niger*, the Christmas rose. It thrives in shady areas, lighting them up with large white flowers with golden stamens, which bloom from midwinter to early spring.

FURTHER READING

ANDERSON, MARY, *Color Healing,* The Aquarian Press, 1979

CAYCE, EDGAR, *Auras, An Essay on the Meaning of Colors,* A.R.E Press, 1973

CHIAZZARI, SUZY, *The Complete Book of Color,* Element, 1998

DALICHOW, IRENE and BOOTH, MIKE, *Aura-Soma,* Hay House Inc., 1996

GIMBEL, THEO, *Healing Through Color,* The C.W. Daniel Company Ltd., 1980

GIMBEL, THEO, *The Color Therapy Workbook,* Element, 1993

GRAHAM, HELEN, *Healing with Color,* Newleaf, 1996

HOLBECHE, SOOZI, *The Power of Gems and Crystals,* Piatkus, 1989

KELLY, JOHN, *The All-Seasons Garden,* Windward, 1987

LACY, MARIE LOUISE, *Know Yourself Through Color,* The Aquarian Press, 1989

LACY, MARIE LOUISE, *The Power of Color to Heal the Environment,* Rainbow Bridge Publications, 1996

OUSELEY, S.G.J., *Color Meditations,* L.N. Fowler & Co. Ltd., 1949

POLUNIN, MIRIAM, *Healing Foods,* Dorling Kindersley, 1997

SUN, HOWARD & DOROTHY, *Color Your Life,* Piatkus, 1998

VERNER-BONDS, LILIAN, *Color,* Southwater, 1999

WALL, VICKY, *The Miracle of Color Healing,* Thorsons, 1995

WAUTERS, AMBIKA and THOMPSON, GERRY, *Principles of Color Healing,* Thorsons, 1997

WILLS, PAULINE, *Working With Color,* Hodder & Stoughton, 1999

USEFUL ADDRESSES

Aura-Soma US Inc.
Will and Trish Hunter
PO Box 1688
Canyon Lake, TX
78130
Tel: (210) 935 2355
Fax: (210) 935 2508

The Color Association of
the United States
589 Eighth Avenue
New York
NY 10018-3005
Tel: (212) 372 000
Website:
www.colorassociation.com

The Hygeia College of
Color Therapy
Brook House
Avening
Tetbury
Glos.
GL8 8NS
UK.
Tel: 01453 832150.
Fax: 01453 835757.
Website:
www.rowantree.co.uk/info
/hygeia

IAC, International
Association of Color
46 Cottenham Road
Histon
Cambridge
CB4 9ES
UK.
Tel: 01223 563403.
Email:
michael@kgrevis.freeserve.
co.uk

Aura-Soma Products Ltd.
South Road
Tetford
Horncastle
Lincs.
LN9 6QB
UK.
Tel: 01507 533581.
Fax: 01507 533412.
Email: info@aura-
soma.co.uk
Website: www.aura-
soma.com

Index

ACKNOWLEDGMENTS

I wish to thank Dolores for all she has taught me over the years; my sister Felicité, and Zena, for their help; and Anne, for her delicious recipes and especially for her support and encouragement.

The publisher would like to thank Helene Enahoro, Ian Louis-Fernand, Helen Furbear, Elizabeth Gough, Tara Grant, Emma Hockridge, J. Kinchett, Ben Lacey, Karen Legg, Kay Macmullan, Janina Sanders, Lorraine Torres, for help with photography.

PICTURE ACKNOWLEDGMENTS

Every effort has been made to trace copyright holders and obtain permission. The publishers apologize for any omissions and would be pleased to make any necessary changes at subsequent printings.
AKG, London: 14B, 18B; /Erich Lessing,18T.
The Bridgeman Art Library, London 58B Wolverhampton Art Gallery, **Corbis, London** 34B Michael Busselle; 62B, 84, 184 Bettmann; 66B Louis Ellen Frank; 70T W. Wayne Lockwood; 70B Art e Immagini SRL; 80 Gary Chowanetz-Elizabeth Whiting Assoc;134B, 207T Eric Crichton;122 Andrew Cowin-Travel Inc. **The Image Bank, London** 79T, 79B, 157, 191, 206T, 215. **Images Colour Library, London** 78B, 142, 145, 158T, 158B, 158–159, 162T, 166, 170, 178, 202 both, 203 both, /Pat O'Hara, 211. **NASA** 30–31 ALL. **The Stock Market, London** 26, 50, 121, 137, 198, 210B, 214B. **Stone/Getty One, London** 15, 21, 42, 46, 54B, 78T, 86–87, 102T, 102B, 138, 180, 190–191, 195, 206B. **Superstock, London** 83.